NICOLA STOW is a bestselling and award-nominated writer, the co-author of a number of books, which have received hundreds of five-star Amazon reviews. These include *One Chance: Surviving London's Gangs*, *No Safe Place: Murdered by our father*, *Above and Beyond: Secrets of a Private Flight Attendant* and *Cabin Fever: The Sizzling Secrets of a Virgin Air Hostess*. She has over twenty years of experience as a journalist, covering crime, news and investigations. She has written for numerous national publications and websites including the *Sun*, *Daily Mail* (Scotland), *Sunday Mail*, *Sunday Post*, *Daily Record*, *The Times*, the *News of the World* and women's magazines, such as *Take a Break and That's Life*.

NICOLA STOW

The Real-Life MURDER Clubs

CITIZENS SOLVING
TRUE CRIMES

AL
AD LIB

First published in 2022 by Ad Lib Publishers Ltd
15 Church Road
London SW13 9HE
www.adlibpublishers.com

Text © 2022 Nicola Stow

Paperback ISBN 978-1-802470-79-6
eBook ISBN 978-1-802470-89-5

A CIP catalogue record for this book is available from the
British Library.

Every reasonable effort has been made to trace copyright-
holders of material reproduced in this book, but if any have
been inadvertently overlooked the publishers would be glad to
hear from them.

Printed in the UK
10 9 8 7 6 5 4 3 2 1

In loving memory of Clive Dennier – a rare beauty of a man.

Contents

Glossary

autopsy – The dissection and examination of a dead body to establish the cause of death and to evaluate diseases or injuries for research and educational purposes. The procedure, also known as post-mortem examination or necropsy, is performed by a pathologist.

bioinformatics – Describes the science of storing, retrieving and analysing large amounts of biological data. It involves using computer technology to collect, store and publish biological information like DNA and amino acid sequences or annotations of sequences.

cold case – An unsolved criminal investigation that remains open pending new evidence.

composite sketch – A police drawing of a suspect based on descriptions from witnesses that could help identify or eliminate said suspect.

data mining – The process of analysing large databases to generate new information.

EARONS – An acronym for East Area Rapist (EAR) and Original Night Stalker (ONS), nicknames coined by the media for the killer-rapist who terrorised California, known as the Golden State, in the seventies and eighties – before he was renamed the Golden State Killer and identified as Joseph DeAngelo.

endangered runaway – The National Center for Missing and Exploited Children defines an endangered runaway as a child under eighteen who's missing and whose whereabouts are unknown to their parents or legal guardians.

endogamy – When many people from a small population have married within that population over many years, making it difficult for genealogists to establish how people are related to one another.

exhume – To remove a dead body from the ground post burial, particularly to extract DNA evidence.

family tree – A chart showing members of different generations of a family and their relationship to one another.

genetic genealogy – Combining genealogical DNA tests and profiling with traditional genealogical methods to establish genetic relationships between people.

GSK – Abbreviation for Golden State Killer, Joseph DeAngelo.

human genome – A human being's complete set of DNA encoded in the twenty-three chromosome pairs in cell nuclei and in a DNA molecule found in individual mitochondria.

IP address – IP is an acronym of Internet Protocol, the rules governing the format of data sent online. An IP address identifies a device on the internet, making it accessible for communication.

Jane and John Does – Law enforcement agencies in America use placeholder names Jane and John (for males) Doe for unidentified corpses.

mandible – Human lower jawbone that holds the bottom teeth in place. An important bone that helps in the identification of remains.

Midazolam – One of three drugs used in a lethal injection. Midazolam knocks the prisoner unconscious.

mitochondrial DNA analysis – Used by forensic scientists when samples such as bones, teeth and hairs without follicles are collected from crime scenes. A mitochondrial DNA test (mtDNA test) traces a person's matrilineal or mother-line ancestry using his or her mitochondria.

Mother Lode – Nickname coined by independent detectives Paul Haynes and Michelle McNamara to describe forty years' evidence relating to the crimes of the Golden State Killer.

MySpace – The most popular social networking site between 2005 and 2008.

Palynology – The study of spores and pollen grains.

Ping map – A tracking chart based on mobile phone evidence to pinpoint a person's whereabouts at given times.

potassium chloride – The third, and final, drug used to stop a prisoner's heart in a lethal injection.

reconstruction – A term used to describe a clay model or sketch of a dead, unidentified victim.

sequenced DNA – A massive, compressed text file detailing base-pairings of ACTG (an acronym for the four bases found in a DNA molecule – adenine, cytosine, thymine and guanine).

State sunshine laws – The laws in individual US states that govern public access to governmental records. They are collectively known as FOIA laws, after the federal Freedom of Information Act.

sock-puppet account – A fictitious social media identity created to deceive others.

The 5150 – A violent gang formed around 2003 in the LA Sierra region of Riverside, California. The gang terrorised the community and, within three years, had committed a plethora of offences from assaults and stabbings to murders.

vecuronium bromide – A drug in a lethal injection which stops the inmate from breathing.

victim impact statement – A written account read in court outlining how a victim has been affected by a crime. A victim impact statement is presented at the sentencing of the defendant.

Introduction

Have you ever come home from work and thought, *Tonight I'll scour the internet, see if I can identify that decayed head found in a bucket of cement?* Or worked through the night drawing digital pictures from autopsy photographs of an unidentified teenager found murdered in a field thirty years ago? Has it ever occurred to you to compare lists of unidentified corpses with those of missing people? If not, then welcome to the surprising world of citizen sleuths.

When asked to write this book, I half-wondered whether I'd find myself discussing a murder or two over tea and cake with a group of candyfloss-haired pensioners – much like the characters in Richard Osman's *The Thursday Murder Club*. But unlike Osman's fictional depiction of citizens solving crimes, the real version, I discovered, is grittier, inhabited by obsessive, intrepid souls who delve into some of the most gruesome cases in true crime history, while seeking justice and truth for both loved ones and strangers.

The real-life citizen sleuths dedicate thousands of hours of their spare time, usually around their day jobs, searching the internet for clues that might lead to a breakthrough in a cold murder case, or help them to find a missing person. They create family trees and pore over court records, police reports, court documents and databases dedicated to the dead and missing – hoping to give names back to victims buried in unmarked graves.

The lengths to which some of these 'armchair detectives' go in their pursuit of answers astounded me. Take Todd Matthews, a former factory worker from Tennessee (you'll meet him later in the book). He spent almost eleven years searching for a name for a dead woman known only as 'Tent Girl', nicknamed after the canvas circus bag that imprisoned her decayed, eyeless corpse. Todd's obsession led to him sleepwalking around his home, armed with a butcher's knife, haunted by visions of Tent Girl's decomposed face.

Another 'internet sleuth' in this book even considered luring her daughter's killers to a remote spot and shooting them throughout her decade-long fight for justice. While a duo on a mission to unmask a serial killer pulled off an *Oceans Eleven*-inspired 'heist' at a county sheriff's office. It's all just another day at the office for the ordinary people solving extraordinary crimes.

Over the last few months, I've got to know some of these sleuths pretty well and, as a journalist, I was hugely impressed by their investigative skills and vast forensic knowledge – I think I've probably learned a thing or two in the process. My Google search history now includes phrases like, 'What happens when a bullet enters your head from behind?', 'What are the three chemicals used in lethal injections?', 'Did the Golden State Killer have a small penis?', 'What does burning flesh smell like?', and, 'How does bioinformatics work?'

Many of my interviewees relayed personal, tragic stories that inspired their journeys into sleuthing. They were generous with their time, a fascinating bunch, so I'll let them – and you – crack on now, as I introduce: the citizen sleuths.

1

Why Did You Kill Her?

Pierce Brothers Crestlawn Memorial Park and Mortuary, Riverside, California, 8 March, 2006

'How could they do this . . . why did they do this to you, baby girl?' Violent sobs jolt in Belinda Lane's chest. She can't feel her legs or her husband's arm around her ribs, holding her up. But she's aware of the pulse of her blood giving life to the wooden mother and child figurine she's cradling which trembles with every beat of her heart. A single red rose flutters in her other hand. Words clog in Belinda's throat as she bows over the pink casket carrying the body of her twenty-four-year-old daughter, Crystal Theobald. 'How . . . could . . . they?'

Slices of afternoon sun from the windows criss-cross the chapel of rest, bathing Crystal's face in peachy light. She's wearing her favourite black lace top and plaid trousers, mahogany hair falling over her shoulders, down to her waist. Red and pink rose stems, left by friends and relatives, lay with her. She looks beautiful, *thinks Belinda, her own face soaked with tears. Slowly, she unfurls her left arm and nestles the figurine in the coffin alongside her daughter. Then she gently places the rose on Crystal's chest.*

With her husband still steadying her, she reaches into the casket. Brushing the back of her hand over Crystal's cheek, Belinda notes the bruise circling her right eye. The injury barely shows – its horror is masked by ivory foundation. But it's there. Belinda sees it through the mist in her eyes, and noises suddenly shatter inside her mind: the crack-crack-crack-crack-crack *of gunfire, an explosion of glass, the shriek of rubber grazing tarmac as an SUV speeds away. The noises will never leave Belinda – they haunt her day and night, playing a devastating soundtrack of* that *evening . . . the evening that somebody killed her daughter.*

Belinda lowers her wet face into the casket, eyes closed as she kisses Crystal's cheek one last time. 'I'm gonna get them, baby girl,' she chokes. 'I will get the people who did this to you – even if it takes me until my dying breath. I love you, baby girl.'

Crystal's funeral took place twelve days after that horrific night in Riverside, when a gunman jumped out of a white Ford Expedition SUV and opened fire on the Honda Civic Crystal was travelling in along with her brother, Justin, and their friend, Juan Patlan. It happened just yards from her house, in her street.

The SUV, a luminous streak pounding gangster rap from the radio, skidded to a diagonal stop between Belinda's car nearby and the Honda Civic carrying her children and their friend. Interior lights splashed on as a door of the SUV was flung open, coughing out the hooded figure of a young man. Hands buried in the pockets of his jacket, he shambled up the kerb then stood still beneath a streetlight and a sign warning, 'STOP'.

Belinda clocked his face: babyish, possibly Hispanic. His jaw was grinding – as though he was chewing a tough lump of steak. Shoulders hunched, he reached into his jacket and pulled a gun from his waist. Belinda instinctively ducked down – the gunman was pointing his weapon right at her – no more than a lorry-length of space separated them. The sound of shots studded the night – two, three, four, five, but no bullets hit Belinda's car. Silence, then *slap-thud, slap-thud, clunk*. Wheels screeched, an engine snarled, then diminished to a hum as the SUV sped into the distance. Belinda lifted her head, a sudden pain slashing her heart. *Oh my God, the kids.*

Crystal had been shot in the head. Juan had also taken a bullet to his stomach. Crystal later died in hospital. The three had been attacked by gangsters in a tragic case of mistaken identity. Whoever they were, they didn't know Crystal, but Belinda, as she vowed on the day of her daughter's funeral, would make it her mission to find them and win justice for her girl who'd brought 'nothing but joy to everybody who knew her.' This tireless quest would consume her for the next ten years.

Even today, sixteen years after the shooting, the grief of losing Crystal is still raw in Belinda's heart. How anyone could kill her beautiful daughter – a mum herself to two little girls – is the unanswerable question Belinda asks herself every day.

Speaking with Belinda, I'm deeply moved by her unwavering love for Crystal and the lengths to which she went to hunt her killers. But, before hearing about Belinda's quest for the truth, I want to know more about the striking woman in the photograph she shows me – a picture of the daughter that proved instrumental in this mum-of-five's fight for justice.

In the photograph, Crystal gazes over her shoulder, head tilted towards the camera, a smile playing on her raspberry-painted lips. She's wearing a summery halter neck top, patterned with royal blue flowers. 'She's stunning,' I say. 'She looks just like a model.' Belinda's eyes well a little as a smile, loaded with memories, fills her face.

'Crystal was my sunshine, my life,' she says. 'It's hard to find words to describe her but, to me, she was just the most beautiful girl in the world. She was a joy, a breath of fresh air. Crystal would give you the shirt off her back – she was so kind and selfless. And, you know, the pain doesn't go away. Sometimes, that night [of the shooting] feels like only yesterday. I still hear the gunshots. I hear the explosion of metal and glass, the screech of wheels and think, why my baby girl?'

Crystal was Belinda's fourth child with her first husband, Robert Theobald, who passed away when Crystal was a young girl. Crystal had three older brothers, Robert, Curtis and Justin. In 1991, Belinda married her current husband, Ben Mariotti, with whom she has another son, Nicholas.

'The day I gave birth to my little girl was one of the happiest moments of my life,' recalls Belinda. 'I adore my sons, but – oh – I was desperate for a little girl.' Belinda describes Crystal as a 'good kid' who did 'really well in school.' 'She loved adventures – heights and rollercoasters,' her mother recalls.

In 2003, Crystal married her boyfriend, Joe Valencia and the pair had two daughters, Angelina and Elizabeth. The girls were just two and fourteen months old respectively when they lost their mother.

Crystal and Joe's marriage started out well. They set up a successful air-conditioning and heating business, funded by Crystal after she got lucky in a Vegas casino one day. Belinda laughs as she remembers the story. 'She went to a slot machine, put in five dollars and won thirty-eight thousand dollars. She and her husband set up the business and, well, they just took off with it.'

But in 2005, the couple's relationship had deteriorated. 'He [Joe] had a history of drug use, and he fell back into that lifestyle. Crystal was heartbroken but she knew she had to get away. So, she and the girls came back home to live with us,' says Belinda.

Leaving her husband heralded a fresh start for Crystal. She enrolled on a nurse-training course at Riverside City College. After a tumultuous year, Crystal finally felt happy and settled – and she was fulfilling her childhood dream. 'Crystal always wanted to be a nurse. She would have made a wonderful nurse as she was such a caring, thoughtful person. A people person. Full of fun, too.'

Friday, 24 February, 2006, is engraved in Belinda's mind as the date her world fell apart. 'Y'know, I remember every second of that day leading up to the shooting,' she tells me. It was a day that turned from joy to tragedy 'in a blink of an eye.'

'It was a regular Friday,' Belinda says. Early evening, after Crystal dropped her daughters at her ex-mother-in-law's house for the weekend, Belinda and Crystal went for a meal at their local KFC restaurant. Over popcorn chicken and fries, the pair chatted excitedly about their plans for the next day. Belinda had recently received a tax rebate, which she'd decided to spend on a new car for Crystal. 'Crystal was so excited; I'd told her how I wanted to spend my tax refund. I said, "Crystal, honey, tomorrow I'm taking you out and you're going to choose a car. I got myself a tax refund and I want to invest it in you." Oh, I tell you, she gave me the cutest smile and she hugged me real tight. I couldn't wait to take Crystal out to buy that car the next day and . . .' Belinda's lips tighten. Her eyes close behind tortoiseshell glasses. 'Well, sweetie,' she resumes, her hand pressed over her heart, 'that didn't happen.'

Belinda first noticed the white Ford Expedition around 8.30 p.m. when she and Crystal returned to their bungalow on Geranium Place, in the Arlanza neighbourhood of Riverside. 'It [the Ford Expedition] looked like it was circuiting the area. It passed our house, the stereo blasting. I guessed they were kids, maybe a gang. There's a lot of gang activity in Riverside, so we're used to seeing stuff like that.'

She and Crystal were only indoors for ten or fifteen minutes before they went out again. 'Crystal wanted some cigarettes and needed to change a hundred-dollar bill, so we decided to go to the 7-Eleven, just a few blocks away. Justin and Juan said they'd come too, so we agreed to take two cars,' says Belinda, adding that, contrary to media reports, Juan was not Crystal's boyfriend. 'I left first in my car, and the others followed in the Civic Honda.'

As she walked across the driveway to her car, the white Ford Expedition SUV drove past Belinda again. 'Every seat in that car was filled,' she recalls. The Expedition cruised on, up to the junction where Geranium Place meets Greenpoint Avenue. Belinda was heading in the same direction. She turned right off her driveway onto Geranium Place. Ahead, the SUV hooked right onto Greenpoint Avenue. In Belinda's rear-view mirror she could see the Honda Civic. All three were in the front seats, with Crystal in the middle and Juan at the wheel.

When she reached the junction, the SUV reappeared to her right, and swerved to a stop. 'I swung left around the Expedition, onto Greenpoint Avenue and quickly turned the car around so I could see what was going on with the kids. The Expedition was angled between me and the Honda. Then I saw the man on the corner, and then I saw him take out the gun. I ducked down fast and waited, expecting him to fire at my car.

'I heard the first bullet hit glass, then at least four or five more shots. I didn't know then that I was listening to my kids' car getting shot up. I didn't even know Crystal had been hit at this point. After the SUV sped away, the kids took off in the Honda. I tried to follow but took a wrong turn and lost them.'

Belinda headed home, unaware that, at the same time, wounded Juan was pulling up outside the nearby Cardenas Markets grocery store. But she would later see the harrowing CCTV footage that captured Justin on his knees on the supermarket's forecourt with Crystal, unconscious, in his arms as he cradled her bleeding head against his chest.

It was just after 9 p.m. when Belinda arrived home to a street strewn with cop cars. Officers had started cordoning the junction at Geranium Place and Greenpoint Avenue with yellow ribbons screaming, 'CRIME SCENE DO NOT CROSS', over and over and over. Belinda found a space to park and got out of the car, her legs like empty cartons. She heard her fourteen-year-old son Nicholas before she saw him. Trainers thumping across concrete, his voice high and panicky: 'Mum, Crystal's been shot . . . Crystal's been shot.'

Belinda's hand flutters to her chest again when she tells me what happened next. 'I just fell to my knees. I screamed, "I have to get to my daughter," slamming my hands on the pavement. Nicholas helped me up and into the house, but the next few minutes are still hazy in my mind. Police officers were there. Ben was trying to comfort me – he'd called 911 when he'd heard the shooting.

'I was starting to feel real sick and the officers were firing all these questions at me, but all I could say was, "Where's my daughter? Take me to my daughter." All the voices blurred around me. Somebody said Juan had also been shot but Justin, miraculously, was uninjured. Cardenas was mentioned. Then, when I heard Riverside Community Hospital, I was gone. I had to get to Crystal. I ran out of the house, got in the car and put my foot down. I drove right through the police tape. Nothing or nobody was gonna stop me getting to my baby girl.'

There were more police officers at the hospital, guarding the room in which Crystal lay. Her head was bandaged and her upper body emmeshed with wires and tubes. A heart monitor bleeped on the offbeat to the steady puffs of the life-support machine. Justin was at her bedside, T-shirt saturated with his sister's blood.

'I died inside when I saw Crystal. She was in a huge private room, like the ones you see on the television show, *ER*, and hooked to a life-support machine. It was horrific.' Belinda's voice is paper-doll thin as she recalls this moment. She lets out a slow intake of breath, then continues, 'Justin was covered in

Crystal's blood. It's a miracle that he didn't get hit. Juan had gone into surgery and he was going to be just fine. But Crystal's condition was critical. The doctors said they needed to do a test to find out whether her brain had died. I held Crystal's hand and said, "Please be OK, baby girl. I can't live without you".'

Belinda stayed at Crystal's bedside through the night, weeping into the early hours and 'praying for a miracle'. At 5 a.m. Belinda had started to feel unwell. Her heart raced and a vice-like headache that had started at the hospital was getting worse by the minute. She decided to go home to change. When she returned to the hospital, the doctor delivered the news she'd been praying she'd never hear. 'I'm sorry, Crystal's brain has gone,' he told her. 'The life-support machine is keeping her alive just now. Whether or not you wish to withdraw this support is entirely your decision. We want to assure you we . . .' But as he spoke, a mottled grey mist blanketed Belinda's eyes. Her head felt like it had turned to concrete. The doctor was still speaking but she could no longer hear him. He became a fuzzy shape in the mist, like the outline of a figure on an old, untuned black-and-white television. Fading, fading, gone.

'I just collapsed into a chair when the doctor told me that,' says Belinda. 'I passed out. Then they rushed me down to the emergency room.'

Tests revealed Belinda had suffered a mild heart attack. 'I had no idea I was having a heart attack. I remember the doctor in ER told me: "I would classify this as broken heart syndrome. You can die of a broken heart, you know." Yeah, I believed him. He said I would need an operation to insert stents in my heart. But there was only one person on my mind at that point – Crystal.'

That evening, Belinda made the hardest decision of her life. 'No mother should have to ask for her child's life support machine to be switched off. But I had to make that decision, for Crystal. And that killed me. They switched off Crystal's machine and she died in my arms. I held her real tight and cried and cried. I told her I love her, that I couldn't live without her – and that's when I first promised her, "I'm gonna get the people who did this to you, baby girl – and they are gonna pay".'

As Crystal drifted away, a deluge of grief filled the hospital room, hollow howls replaced the bleeps of hope that had come before. Belinda cried into her daughter's hair. 'I miss you, baby girl.'

Belinda would wait six months before surgeons operated on her 'broken' heart.

* * *

Belinda knew who was behind the shooting that led to her daughter's death before the day of Crystal's funeral. Her son, Nicholas, had heard whisperings in the neighbourhood about the involvement of the 5150 – a gang embroiled in violent turf wars with rival mobsters in the area.

According to Urban Dictionary, 5150 is police code for 'crazy one on the loose' who is 'a danger to property', 'a danger to others', and 'a danger to themselves'. It is also a term used to describe someone who's 'willing to put their life on the line'. The 5150 gang formed around 2003 in the LA Sierra region of Riverside. Within three years, they had committed a plethora of offences from assaults and stabbings to murders and were terrorising the community.

On the night of Crystal's murder, the 5150 were apparently searching for a rival gang who called themselves MD. Julio 'Lil Huero' Heredia, of the 5150 gang, wanted to 'take out' MD members who were allegedly planning to kill one of his fellow gangsters. That night, those members of MD were driving a car which was like the one driven by Juan.

Nicholas was convinced the 5150 gang had murdered his sister. He believed that, during a chase that night, the 5150 lost track of the car carrying the MD targets. When they saw the Honda Civic carrying Juan, Justin and Crystal on Geranium Place, they assumed they'd found their targets and opened fire on the vehicle. Nicholas had found information about the 5150 and their activities on the, now defunct, social media platform, MySpace. He alerted his then fourteen-year-old cousin, Jaimie McIntyre to his findings. Jaimie was also determined to win justice for her beloved cousin.

Belinda had felt the Riversdale Police Department's investigation into Crystal's murder was moving 'too slow'. Aside from a shoe and several bullet casings found at the scene, no further evidence had come to light in the aftermath of the shooting. 'I'd made a promise to Crystal that I would find her killers and make them pay, so that's what I was going to do,' she tells me, her voice taking on a defiant tone now. 'I had the names for those gang members before my daughter was in the ground. I knew one of them was William "Jokes" Sotelo, who drove a white Ford Expedition SUV. And I knew he was the getaway driver on the night of the shooting. I just had to prove this.'

Belinda and Jaimie decided to set up a fake profile and befriend as many members of the 5150 as possible in an effort to find the individual responsible for Crystal's death. Belinda had not used social media until now. She explains that Jaimie set up the profile. 'She found this picture of a young pretty woman in a Supergirl T-shirt, so we named her Rebecca and created a profile on MySpace. This was all new to me, but Jaimie was young and knew how to speak with these people. Jaimie asked me what I wanted her to do with Rebecca. I told her, "Get as much information as you can."'

Jaimie set up Rebecca's page, painting her as a fun-loving partygoer from Riverside. Rebecca was 'five-foot-two', 'curvy' and, most importantly, 'single'. Her profile said that she liked to 'hang out with friends and my girlfriends, smoke weed, drink cervezas, [and] dance my ass off.' Rebecca's music tastes included R&B singer Usher, rap artist 50 Cent, hip-hop duo Outkast, Avril Lavigne and some 'oldies'.

Posing as Rebecca, Jaimie found dozens of gang members, who were often showing off their 5150 tattoos in their profile pictures. She clicked on their names, added their profiles to her 'top 8' – a MySpace feature that allowed users to rank their eight favourite friends – on Rebecca's page. Soon, the woman in the Supergirl T-shirt had 150 gang member friends.

Jaimie would spend hours after school each night, sending private messages to the 5150 men. Rebecca used teasing, youthful street slang. 'Whadup?' she wrote to one named 'lil eazzzzzy'. 'You'd like my homegirls,' she told another called 'Charlie'. 'We should hang out sometime ;),' Rebecca suggested to Antonio.

Belinda followed the exchanges on her laptop. 'We were just trying to figure out where these guys were from, what they were doing. I kept asking Jaimie to ask them about the white Ford Expedition, but Jaimie said she needed to "play it out" with these guys first.'

But one day in March 2006, Belinda's impatience got the better of her. Undoubtedly, the 5150 members liked Rebecca, but they weren't offering up the information Belinda wanted. She asked Jaimie to create a second profile using the picture of Crystal in her halter top. 'Rebecca wasn't getting us enough hits,' Belinda explains. 'So, I said, let's get Crystal's picture up there. So that's what we did. I wanted these guys to fall in love with Crystal.'

Belinda wrote the profile for the new MySpace account using her daughter's picture, and she chose the name 'Angel'. 'I will be your biggest life mistake and your deepest, darkest, best-kept secret,' Angel promised. Angel's page glittered with rose and heart animations. 'Dynamite comes in small packages,' she professed, 'I've got a lot of love to give so if you're cool say hi.'

Messages flooded Angel's MySpace inbox, including several from the 5150 member Belinda had hoped to snare: William 'Jokes' Sotelo. Jokes was into 'porn' and 'scary movies', according to his page. Below his profile picture, which showed him posturing in sunglasses and low-slung jeans, he boasted: 'IE ryder for life on the real 5150 is down to kill.'

An online rapport grew between Angel and Jokes. 'We [as Angel] told Jokes that her mum was in jail for cooking meth. I thought that would get him to open up a bit about prison and drugs, but the opposite happened. It got deep. He was like, "I'm sorry about that, I'm here for you".' Jokes was clearly falling for Angel. 'I can't stop thinking about you,' he said in another message.

He invited her to a party, and she accepted – although Belinda and Jaimie agreed that Angel should pull out of the occasion 'at the last minute'. This she did, messaging Jokes to explain, 'I can't find a ride.'

'I'll pick you up,' offered Jokes. This was exactly the response Belinda had hoped to hear.

The exchange continued. 'If you were to come and pick me up, what kinda car am I supposed to look for?' asked Angel.

'My white Ford Expedition,' he wrote.

Belinda contacted the detective who was heading the investigation into Crystal's murder. 'As soon as we got that message from Jokes, I got on the phone to Detective Rick Wheeler. I said, "I think we've found them." I told him about 5150, Jokes's messages and about the MySpace account. I think he was pretty taken aback at what we'd been doing.'

Police acted on Belinda's information and traced William 'Jokes' Sotelo. He attended a voluntary interview, in which he incriminated Julio Heredia as the gunman who shot Crystal and Juan – but vehemently denied being present himself on the night of the murder. Detective Wheeler knew Sotelo was lying but, at this stage, investigators didn't have enough evidence to hold him in custody, so they had to let him go.

In April 2006, Jaimie stepped down from the MySpace campaign and handed Angel's page over to her aunt. 'It became too much for Jaimie,' says Belinda. 'I understood this. Jaimie was very close to Crystal.

'I took over the page. I was depressed at this point, furious that Sotelo had been let go. Oh, I got angry on that MySpace page. I went all out to catch Sotelo. I messaged the gang members, asking them direct questions about their families, asking where they lived. I drove past their houses, took pictures of their vehicles, noted all the number plates. I dropped voodoo dolls in their yards. I called the FBI, tried to get them all deported. Detective Wheeler told me to back off. He said a lot of white Ford Expeditions were getting torched all over Riverside. But the last thing I was going to do was back off. I wanted justice for Crystal. I missed her so much. I was still expecting her to walk through the door.'

Belinda's grief and rage led her to have some violent thoughts. Her focus had now shifted from simply finding her daughter's killers to exacting revenge on all 5150 gang members. One day she found herself thinking, '*If I can get them all to a remote spot, I can shoot them all.*' She decided Angel should throw a party to reel them in. Belinda posted on Angel's MySpace page, inviting her 5150 contacts to an 'end of the world' party on 6 June, 2006. She told the gang members that a location for the event would be confirmed nearer the time. 'Oh, I was about to shoot them all. I didn't know what I was thinking. I had a gun – I don't have one now – and I was going to kill them. Luckily, my husband and boys made me see sense. I realised then, that I wouldn't kill them. But I still wanted to find Jokes Sotelo.'

On the eve of the fake party, Belinda returned to MySpace and sent another message to Jokes from Angel's account. 'You're still on here?' asked Angel.

'Can't wait to see you at the party tomorrow,' he replied instantly. Belinda burst into tears. *Does he know who he's speaking to? Does he not recognise Angel, this beautiful girl in the photograph? I want him to hurt like we're hurting,'* were Belinda's thoughts as her fingers trembled over the keys.

'I know who you are,' she typed. 'Do you love me?'

'ha u know I do,' he shot back.

Tears streamed over Belinda's chin and dripped onto her keyboard. She took a sharp breath and wrote, 'Then why did you kill me? This is Crystal Theobald. I'm the girl you murdered.'

Belinda didn't stop there. 'I sat at my computer and cried and cried and cried. I carried on messaging Jokes. I asked him again, "Why did you kill me?" I said, "You don't even know who you killed. You're looking at Crystal's picture as Angel. You killed her. She's gone. Why did you kill me? I had dreams, I had hopes. Why?" Well, Jokes didn't respond to that and, shortly after, he went on the run. He fled the country. I handed the MySpace over to Detective Wheeler after I confronted Jokes. I had to – to keep myself in check.'

* * *

A year passed with no news on Sotelo's whereabouts. Although she'd relinquished Angel's MySpace account to Detective Wheeler, Belinda refused to give up on her one-woman mission to find him. She scanned other social media sites like Facebook and Twitter and kept an eye on the 5150 members' activity on MySpace, but the gang's online presence had diminished amid the ongoing police investigation. Belinda spoke regularly with Detective Wheeler, and, on 8 August, 2007, he called her with the news she'd been longing to hear. The investigator had identified two other 5150 gang members, William 'Rascal' Lemus and his brother Manuel 'Tripper' Lemus, who were in the Ford Expedition the night of the shooting – and they had provided critical information about the man they claimed fired the gun in exchange for immunity. 'We've just charged Julio Heredia with murder,' said the detective.

'Oh, I was so happy to hear this,' Belinda tells me, smiling. 'Nothing could bring Crystal back, but, at last, the person who took her from me would face justice.'

Heredia stood trial in 2011. He was set to face the death penalty, and Belinda initially fought for this, but she later asked for this punishment to be removed. 'It seemed like the right decision. I did the right thing for the first time in my life,' she admits. During the trial, the Lemus brothers testified against Heredia. He was found guilty of Crystal's murder and sentenced to life without parole. 'I just hope he lives a very long life,' Belinda says.

Life carried on for Belinda, but not a day went by when she didn't think about her vow to find *every* gang member who was inside the Ford Expedition on the evening of 24 February, 2006. Every time she visited Crystal's grave Belinda would repeat this promise aloud: 'I will get the people who did this to you – even if it takes me until my dying breath. I love you, baby girl.'

At times, Belinda thought she would never find Sotelo again. But, in 2014, while searching on Facebook, Belinda finally got her breakthrough. There he was, William 'Jokes' Sotelo, masquerading behind a fake name. He'd even posted Crystal's MySpace photograph on his newsfeed. According to Sotelo's page, he was living in Mexico. Excited, she called Detective Wheeler. 'I thought, "*This is it, we've got him.*" But Detective Wheeler said I'd need an exact address for Sotelo in Mexico before the government would consider issuing a warrant. So, I put a small post on the 'What's Happening in Riverside' Facebook group. I wrote, "William Sotelo is still wanted for the first-degree murder of Crystal Theobald. If anyone has any information, there's an award [reward] available." And it all took off from there. I had done millions of posts like this before but this one felt different.'

The next day, Belinda received a private message from a female acquaintance of Sotelo. She directed Belinda to her personal Facebook page. 'I can't send you a friend request as his family can see my profile,' she said. 'But take a look at my page. I know exactly where that son of a bitch is.' Belinda urged the woman to forward this information to Detective Wheeler.

'I gave her his number and pleaded with her. I said, "Please do this for me and I'll owe you my life." Then I called Detective Wheeler myself to tell him the news. I was breathless with excitement. "This is it. This is him, we've got him," I said. Then Detective Wheeler was like, "Hold on, I've got somebody on the other line." It was the woman who'd contacted me. And she gave him Sotelo's address, in Mexico.'

Sotelo was captured in central Mexico on 6 May, 2016, and arrested by state police, who extradited him to the US the next day. By that time, Sotelo was married with four children and had been working as a chili farmer in Mexico. 'I never thought it would take so long to find him. I was naïve in the beginning. When we started the MySpace hunt I thought we'd have caught all of the gang members by the summer. But we got him, at last. Now, I just needed to see him in court.'

That day eventually came in January 2020. Sotelo, after pleading guilty to voluntary manslaughter and gang and firearm charges, stood in the dock at Riverside County Superior Court awaiting his fate. Sotelo had been charged with first-degree murder, but this was dropped in a plea-bargaining deal he struck with prosecutors.

Belinda delivered a victim impact statement, unleashing almost fourteen years of agony. 'I gave Sotelo my hardest stare. Then I let him have it. I called him a punk, a monster, a coward. And I told him, "I hope other gang members snuff your life out while you're in prison." I'd waited a long time to say those words to Sotelo, but he didn't even look sorry. He just stood there, staring at the opposite wall. He couldn't even look at me.' Judge John D. Molloy sentenced Sotelo to twenty-two years in jail. 'I thought this seemed lenient at the time, but I was pleased to see Sotelo behind bars where he belongs.'

After the hearing, Belinda went to Crystal's grave. 'I lay some flowers and said, "We got them, baby girl",' she remembers.

I ask Belinda whether she'd consider visiting Sotelo in jail and, if so, what she would say to him. She thinks for a moment then sighs. 'I don't think he'd want me to visit him but, if I did, I guess the first thing I'd ask is, "Why did you kill her?" He never answered this question before.'

After fulfilling her promise to Crystal, Belinda felt compelled to help other families of murder victims who have yet to win justice for their loved ones. In Crystal's memory, she set up a Facebook page called 'Unsolved Murders in Riverside', where she shares information on cold cases. Belinda runs community events for the group and supports other parents. Her aim, she tells me, is to raise awareness for 'victims seeking justice.' She says, 'I sit down with the mums — there's one here in Riverside just now who's just lost a child to murder – and we chat. I try to guide them through. It seems I've learned a lot along the way. I know how these other mums feel: terrified, horrified. Victims' rights are coming on a little way but we're nowhere near where we should be with them in this country.

'I feel so sorry for parents who never find out who killed their son or daughter. I knew I couldn't rest until I'd found Crystal's killers.'

Belinda and her husband, Ben, are also ambassadors for the One Legacy Foundation, a non-profit organisation dedicated to saving lives through organ donation. Their connection with One Legacy is particularly poignant as Crystal had signed on as a donor. Since her death, Crystal's organs have saved five lives, Belinda informs me. She regularly receives letters from her daughter's organ recipients via One Legacy.

An eighteen-year-old woman received Crystal's lungs. 'Oh, she wrote a beautiful letter,' says Belinda, hands cupping her face. 'She wrote and said that before the surgery, she couldn't breathe or walk, but with Crystal's lungs she could take her dog for walks and play basketball with her boyfriend. She also went to her grandmother's hundredth birthday celebrations.'

Crystal's heart went to an eleven-year-old Riverside boy. 'He'll be twenty-seven soon. I'm told he's a very sweet young man who's doing very well. It just warms *my* heart to know somebody's child got to go home from hospital that day.' Belinda pauses then her smile, radiating fond memories, returns. 'Even in death, Crystal's given life to people. Crystal's the hero of this tragedy – and her heart beats on.'

2

The World's First Cyber-sleuth

Caryville, Campbell County, Tennessee, autumn 2001

The handover of human remains occurs smoothly in the car park outside a Shoney's diner guarded by rusty forested mountains, on the road that leads to Knoxville.

A church-like silence fills Todd Matthews' car as Eddie Barton, in the passenger seat, passes him the item, packaged in a black cloth duffel bag 'I trust you with this, Todd,' he says. 'I think this is the start of something for you. And I believe we'll finally get some answers after all these years.'

As Todd accepts the bundle, a look of excitement beams beneath the peak of his baseball cap. He knows what's inside this small holdall. It's the reason he has driven ninety miles across Tennessee – navigating menacing, winding mountain roads to get here. That said, Todd would have travelled any distance to make this crucial meeting with Eddie.

The skull inside the bag feels lighter than Todd had imagined. He turns to Eddie, one of three detectives who worked on the Campbell County Jane Doe No. 2 murder investigation that has lain cold for four years. Now nearing retirement, Eddie is determined to identify the woman before he hands in his badge.

'I will do everything in my power to bring this woman home to her family,' Todd assures him. With his solid licoricey moustache above a smile so white it dings, Todd resembles a young Burt Reynolds in his Smokey and The Bandit *days. He's not a conventional lawman. Todd has no badge or gun or degree in forensic anthropology. But he does have an impeccable reputation as a 'DIY-detective', as a man committed to naming the nameless and giving faces to the faceless.*

Eddie's habitual careworn expression smooths and lifts. 'It sure would be great to see this case solved. As I said, I've every faith in you, Todd,' he says, popping the handle of the passenger door. 'Have a safe drive back, buddy.'

And now it's just Todd and the human skull of an unnamed woman in the car. He waves through the windshield at the detective, settles the duffel bag in the passenger seat, then slowly drives out of the car park and onto Route 52, heading west through bronzed landscape, homeward bound to Livingston, Tennessee. A citizen sleuth on a mission.

Ten minutes before this macabre exchange, the two friends had sat on facing glossy claret banquettes, engrossed in animated conversation while tucking into the 'all you care to eat' Shoney's lunch buffet. They'd talked about their plans for the object in the bag Eddie Barton had in his car: a female skull with two holes through its temporal bones, marking the points where the bullet entered and exited the dead woman's head.

The victim's naked and decomposing body had been found in October 1998 by a man searching for cans in Stinking Creek, a community in Campbell County – named after its foul-smelling sulphur spring. The autopsy report revealed that the woman was a homicide victim. Her unknown killer had beaten her, plunged a blade into her chest, and shot her in the head.

Over lunch, Eddie and Todd had discussed information gathered so far about the unidentified victim. She was a black woman aged between thirty and forty, with a 'tusky' smile and toenails slicked with toffee apple-red varnish. A wedding band wreathed her left ring finger. She was around five foot and four inches, weighed an estimated nine stone, and had brown hair and eyes. DNA tests yielded no match for either a missing person or a suspect in any crime. Fingerprints obtained from the victim also remained unmatched with any on record. The mutilated woman, who had been left like rubbish at the roadside, was christened Campbell County Jane Doe No. 2 (law enforcement in America use placeholder names Jane and John Doe for unidentified corpses). After the autopsy, County Jane Doe No. 2's hands were sent to the Campbell County Medical Office in Kentucky. Her skull was also retained but the rest of her remains were buried.

Fast forward twenty-one years and I'm gaping at my computer screen as Todd tells me this story as we talk via video call. 'Putting a family back together and making it whole again is very important to me. I don't think detectives release human remains into the custody of a civilian that often,' he says in his looping Tennessee brogue, and I nod rapidly. 'But there was a mutual trust between Eddie and me. He had been trying to solve the case of the woman found murdered near Stinking Creek for years. So, I reached out to him. And in handing over the skull to me I knew Eddie was trying to ensure that his work would be completed.'

Todd contacted the detective after the pair featured in a *Court TV* article together in August 2001. The report, titled 'The Case of the Campbell County Jane Does', chronicled Eddie's investigation into the murders of two women – both unidentified. Jane Doe No. 1, had been found, naked and stabbed to death in the same area as Campbell County Jane Doe No. 2, in January 1997.

The two slayings did not happen in Campbell County, Eddie had concluded. He believed an unknown serial killer probably executed both women elsewhere before dumping their bodies near Stinking Creek. But figuring out where the victims had disappeared from was proving a long struggle for the seasoned detective. Eddie had followed tips that led him to all corners of Tennessee – they took him into crack dens and brothels – but they all came to dead ends.

Casting his net further afield for clues in the two cases, Eddie turned to the FBI's National Crime Information Center (NCIC) database. The computerised index which lists missing people and criminal data, allows law enforcement agencies to exchange information. Here, Eddie could compare the characteristics of the two Jane Does with those of reported missing women.

'There were some distinctive features about Jane Doe No. 1,' explains Todd. 'She was aged between thirty-five and forty-five and believed to be of Hispanic or Native American descent. She had tattoos, too – a rose inked on her inside left elbow, a peacock on her left shoulder and one that read "Mom 77" on her right arm.

'But there was less information for the second Doe as she was quite decomposed – it's thought she was killed a few days before her body was spotted. She had no identifying marks or scars or tattoos. Just an overgrown right front tooth, like a tusk. Both NCIC searches drew blanks.'

As well as outlining the case Eddie had been working on for so many years, the *Court TV* article also lauded Todd's work as media coordinator for the DOE Network, which he co-founded with Jennifer Marra and Helene Wahlstrom in 1999. The volunteer-run organisation is devoted to assisting investigating agencies in bringing closure to cold cases involving missing and unidentified people worldwide. As stated on the DOE Network website's homepage: 'It is our mission to give the nameless back their names and return the missing to their families.'

Todd believed he could help shine a light on the two cold cases via the DOE Network and his new forensic art initiative, Project EDAN. A talented visual artist himself, he launched Project EDAN – an acronym for 'Everyone Deserves a Name' – in February 2001. Working with a group of volunteer certified forensic artists, Todd's mission was to 'give faces to the faceless' by creating composite sketches and clay reconstructions of unidentified victims, based on autopsy photographs and skulls. He remembers well the day he called Eddie to suggest creating a reconstruction of Campbell County Jane Doe No. 2.

'I thought to myself, here we are, two hillbillies together in this *Court TV* article, I'll give him a call. So, I called him and asked, "Have you considered a forensic reconstruction of the 1998 Campbell County Jane Doe?"

'Eddie told me that the authorities would never pay for a forensic artist in this case. "They wrote her off as a crack-addict prostitute who was probably put out of a truck," he said, "It's so frustrating."

'Well, I put it to Eddie: "I can get a reconstruction done for free. Will you let me do this?" And he said, "Yes, absolutely." Eddie told me that he knew about – and valued – my work as a citizen detective and was keen to team-up with me. I was so excited. Over the next couple of months, Eddie and I spoke frequently on the phone, discussing the Campbell County Jane Doe cases at length. I loaded the two Campbell County Jane Does' details onto the DOE Network – which Eddie agreed would give the two cases more visibility. Eddie and I understood one another. We fast became good friends and arranged to meet in Caryville in the fall so I could pick up the remains.'

On the day of the skull handover, before the two gumshoes lunched at Shoney's, they drove out to the locations where the Jane Does' naked bodies had been dumped. From there, they visited the nearby Peabody Cemetery in the Tennessee city of LaFollette, where the Jane Does' graves squatted side by side, both headstones inscribed, 'Unknown'. The solemn vista was familiar to Todd, who'd stood at the gravesides of many unidentified victims in his pursuit to name them. 'Standing in silence in the cemetery, I could tell that Eddie and I shared a strong connection,' he says, 'not only to one another but to the Jane Does too. I knew Eddie was thinking the same as me: *We must bring these women home to their families, so they can be laid to rest beneath gravestones bearing their names.*'

When Todd arrived home that evening, he carefully unpacked the duffel bag and examined the skull. 'It was clean and solid,' he recalls. 'The skull had been bleached – part of the cleaning process of remains from back in the day – which had obviously destroyed a lot of forensic evidence. Aside from the bullet holes, there was no further damage to the skull.'

The next day, Todd made some scaled drawings of Jane Doe No. 2's head – then mailed the skull and his sketches to Wes Neville, a South Carolina-based forensic artist he'd assigned to sculpt a clay bust of Jane Doe. Wes believed Jane Doe's prominent tooth could be a key identifier for her. Therefore, he constructed two busts – one with her mouth closed and the latter showing her smiling.

'These reconstructions are not portraits,' Todd stresses. 'People often look at such images expecting an exact likeness to their loved ones. An educational goal of EDAN is to teach people *how* to view forensic artwork. These pictures are our ghosts, whispers of what a person might have looked like. An echo. The hope with a reconstruction is that it might just trigger people's memories. They might recognise a feature – which is why, with the Campbell County reconstruction, Wes highlighted Jane Doe No. 2's overgrown tooth.'

Weeks later, Wes hand-delivered his smiling Jane Doe sculpture to Todd, who was thrilled with the finished piece.

The artist had expressed Jane Doe's prominent features: her large tooth, jutting jawline, and fleshy cheeks hemmed with the creases of her smile. Her nose is curved slightly to the right, and she wears a cap of tight umber curls. This Campbell County Jane Doe was no longer a brief list of vital statistics. She had a face – one arranged in an inimitable expression at that. Todd was confident Wes's artwork would prompt answers in the three-year mystery – and possibly provide a name for the tragic murder victim. Todd recalls, 'I told Wes, "As soon as I get a name for her, you'll be the first to know. I will make that call." I wanted Wes to know the importance of his artwork.'

Todd posted photographs of the bust on the DOE Network and Project EDAN websites, along with sketches he'd commissioned other forensic artists to make from the clay model. He displayed the sculpture on a shelf in his 'Doe office', a recess he created off his living room, and called her, 'Sally'. 'The nickname stuck. "Sally" became Wes and my reference for the bust. We didn't want to call her "The Girl with a Bullet in her Head".'

Six years rolled by without a positive match for the murdered woman. Although now retired, the case still consumed Eddie. He pored over his bulging folder packed with evidence and expended leads, hoping for something he'd missed – a breakthrough – that would see Jane Doe No. 2 buried with a name. 'These cases, they're like a cancer – kind of eating you,' he told *Knoxville News Sentinel* at the time.

As Todd affirms, keeping the 1998 victim 'on the radar' was critical. 'We needed to make this Doe a permanent memory in the community where she was found and beyond – because she's a homicide victim and she's relevant.'

Fresh hope infused the Campbell County Jane Doe No. 2 case in 2007 when the US government recruited Todd to help create and co-direct the National Missing and Unidentified Persons System (NamUs – pronounced 'Name us'). The Department of Justice system manages an online database of records detailing unidentified bodies, cross-referenced to files on missing people. NamUs was created to support families impacted by the death or disappearance of a loved one, and provide free forensic resources such as fingerprint examination, odontology, anthropology and DNA analysis. Anyone can register case information on the database.

With NamUs established, Todd entered Campbell County Jane Doe No. 2's details into the system, complete with photographs of Wes's clay reconstruction of her and the four versions sketched by the other artists. 'Adding Campbell County Jane Doe No. 2 to NamUs meant we could take advantage of the database's resources. For example, should NamUs obtain fingerprint records that have apparently not been run, it will provide access to the FBI to process the prints.'

As the 1998 Doe's NamUs file went live, the DOE Network and Project EDAN buzzed with incredible news. While creating exposure for the 1998 Doe, Todd had also recruited a forensic artist to draw an impression of Campbell County Jane Doe No. 1. And, in March 2007 a citizen detective had identified her. After a decade resting anonymously, a name could finally be etched on the Doe's gravestone. Her name was Ada Elena Torres Smith, a thirty-two-year-old Hispanic woman last seen in Santee, South Carolina, in June 1996.

'A DOE Network volunteer connected information about a missing woman with the network's file on Campbell County Jane Doe No. 1,' says Todd. 'The missing report contained details about the woman's tattoos, which matched those on Elena. She was then formally identified from fingerprints, which had not been sent to the NCIC but appeared on another database. At last, Ada could be returned to her family.'

Ada's identification fuelled Todd's resolve to find Campbell County Jane Doe No. 2's name, but it became an investigation that would endure for more years. He worked day and night, raked the burgeoning lists of missing people on the DOE Network and NamUs, looking for a woman who bore similar characteristics to the murder victim. When he found potential names, he arranged DNA tests, searched for dental records and more fingerprint evidence. Todd blogged about 'Sally' on his website and seized every opportunity to beam her clay face out to the public via the media. Pictures of the bust were broadcast on ABC's top breakfast television show, *Good Morning America*, which is watched by millions. Still, no match emerged for Sally, but Todd battled on because, 'I will never give up on a case or forget about a Jane or John Doe. When you forget . . . that's when no one remembers them.'

And then, a glimmer of light in the case. In 2015, Todd returned to Peabody Cemetery, where he helped forensic anthropologists dig up Campbell County Jane Doe No. 2's remains for DNA analysis. It took the team two-and-a-half hours to unearth the casket containing only bones. Experts at the Knox County Regional Forensics Center then cleaned up the skeleton and extracted DNA. The lab submitted the genetic material to the FBI's Combined DNA Index System (CODIS), which archives and compares DNA profiles obtained from crime scenes, unidentified bodies, missing people and convicted criminals. Todd felt optimistic that a match might be imminent. 'Exhuming the body meant we could reassemble her. Her remains had been scattered for so many years. Now, we got to interact with all three parts of her – and plug her DNA into CODIS. We finally pushed her together into one agency, which was good. I knew we would identify her soon – and I was all ready to make that promised call to Wes.'

Todd did eventually get to make that call to the artist, but not until February 2022, when he heard the news himself from the Campbell County Sheriff's Office. The skull that Eddie placed in Todd's care almost twenty-one years previously belonged to Lori Alexander from Ohio. The twenty-seven-year-old was reported missing from the city of Toledo in September 1999.

Lori's identification came after the Knox County Regional Forensics Center submitted her fingerprints to a newly updated FBI database. This meant her prints could be compared to recently digitised fingerprint cards from other states from previous decades, and this finally struck a positive match for the young woman.

The victim's name surprised Todd, who had long thought another missing black woman, Pamela Webster Palmer, could be their Jane Doe. 'In a sense her name was very familiar to me as Lori is also my wife's name. But Lori Alexander was not a missing person I'd heard about before. Pamela Webster Palmer, listed on the DOE Network, had seemed a probable match. She was last seen in Raleigh, in Wake County, North Carolina in October 1996.

'But our Campbell County Jane Doe No. 2 had finally been identified. Fingerprints ultimately confirmed that ID but there were a lot of hands that pushed the process along. Wes's reconstruction was pivotal as it gave the case visibility. I texted him right away. I wrote, "I have a name for Sally. I need to make that call." Wes replied immediately. "Call now, brother," he said.'

Authorities returned Lori Alexander's remains to surviving relatives. 'Now it's my mission to find out everything I can about Lori Alexander,' vows Todd. The murders of Ada Elena Torres Smith and Lori Alexander remain under investigation.

* * *

Todd is speaking to me from his lounge in Livingston, Tennessee, a cosy rural town in Overton County where he was born and raised. He has a cheery disposition that belies the impact of death and grief his family endured from when he was an early age. Todd was two when his baby sister, Sue Ann, passed away minutes after her birth. Then, seven years later, his younger brother, Gregory Kenneth, also died when he was just hours old. Both infants suffered birth abnormalities possibly caused after their father, James, was exposed to Agent Orange (a herbicide used as a weapon by the US forces) while serving in the United States Army during the Vietnam War.

Todd's survival was also uncertain. At eight years old he underwent major surgery for a heart defect (coarctation of the aorta). Todd readjusts his beige baseball cap, a look of surprise on his face. 'The doctor stood at my bedside and said to my parents, "This kid won't make it past his teens",' he recalls. 'I always thought that I should have been the sibling who died and, as a child, I felt guilty for surviving. But here I am at fifty-two, still going strong.'

Todd regularly visits Sue and Gregory's graves in the nearby Connor-Pryor Cemetery. 'Our family holds the deeds to Connor-Pryor Cemetery, where my maternal grandmother Della Mae Vaughn [maiden name Pryor] and many of her ancestors are buried. I remember playing among the gravestones as a kid while my father and uncle mowed the lawn. I feel grateful that at least I can visit my siblings and that they can rest peacefully in graves bearing their names.' He still grieves for his siblings but seeing their names inscribed on their tiny headstones gives Todd some comfort – and drives his passion for what he does best: solving the mysteries of the missing and the dead.

Perched on his sofa, chunky golden letters spelling 'WELCOME' on the wall behind, Todd's eyes gloss with nostalgia and the thick broom below his nose climbs with a smile when I bring up the subject of 'Tent Girl'. The name refers to a mystery that endured for more than thirty years, surrounding the identity of a murdered woman who was found wrapped in carnival tent material and ditched in the Kentucky backwoods bordering Eagle Creek near Georgetown. It's a case that would consume Todd for over a decade in an investigation that ultimately earned him fame as the pioneer of cyber-sleuthing. It's a love story of sorts, and it started sometime around Halloween, 1987, at Todd's former high school, Livingston Academy.

In the study hall decked with plastic pumpkins and skeletons and satsuma-coloured garlands, seventeen-year-old Todd sat mesmerised as Lori Riddle, head held casually on one side, told of the day her father stumbled across the canvas-swathed corpse. Lori – a willowy teenager, with a plume of excitable brown curls about her shoulders – had beguiled Todd since he'd first clapped eyes on her a few days ago. He'd spotted Lori, whose family had just moved to town from Scott County, Kentucky, in the school cafeteria. Todd had nudged his friend Jack in the ribs, pointed with his forehead at the girl in the burgundy Kentucky High School jacket, and said, 'That's the girl I'm gonna marry.'

Now, watching Lori's lips expel the macabre scene her dad Wilbur had encountered on 17 May, 1968, Todd was even more enthralled. He loved a mystery, did Todd, and this one hooked him from the get-go.

'One day, my dad found a dead woman in the woods,' began Lori, like she was talking about the weather. 'She'd been tied up in a tent. She was naked and decomposed beyond recognition.' Lori paused, flicked her black coffee eyes at the few students gathered around the table. Until now, the friends had been trying to scare each other with concocted Halloween stories starring zombies, vampires and ghouls. The kind of tales with monsters under the bed – peppered with appropriate sound effects: knuckles going thud, thud, thud on the table, mimicking footsteps; nasal hums for ghosts; a crack of lightning from the back of the throat. But Lori didn't need to dress up her anecdote. It was raw and sad – a real-life horror story. 'Nobody knows the woman's name, so she's known as "Tent Girl",' she finished.

Something about Lori's story resonated with Todd. Although this was the first time he'd heard the grisly tale, Tent Girl seemed somehow familiar to him. He felt a ghost-like connection to her. Reliving his high school memory today, Todd radiates with compassion for the victim who became 'like family' to him. 'As soon as Lori told the story of Tent Girl, I just knew I had to find out her name. This was an important story – and already Tent Girl felt a part of my life. I thought, "*She deserves her real name on her gravestone*."'

When their study hall class ended, Todd walked Lori home and they talked more about Tent Girl. She had been buried in Georgetown Cemetery and Lori told Todd that the woman's gravestone was ornamented with her nickname and engraved with a police sketch depicting how she might have looked in life. She had become an urban legend in Kentucky and some feared the ghost of Tent Girl, said Lori. Students at Georgetown College dared one another to go to her grave at midnight. 'They need to come back with a chalk rubbing of Tent Girl's face from her headstone to prove they were there,' she told Todd. When they reached Lori's home, she cast her classmate a shy smile. 'Do you want to come in and meet my dad?' she asked.

Todd's repaired heart sprinted with delight. 'Sure,' he said. 'I'd love to.' Seconds later, Todd shook hands with the man who'd found Tent Girl.

In the Riddles' sitting room, Todd listened with insurmountable fascination as Wilbur recounted how he'd stumbled upon the girl in the tent nineteen years ago. On that Friday morning in 1968, Wilbur, then working as a water well driller, had turned up for work at a site near Eagle Creek to find a note from his boss: 'Do not start drilling until I arrive.' With time to kill, Wilbur decided to go for a stroll.

Ahead in the distance, miniature figures wriggled atop telephone pylons. *'That'll be the men replacing the Hemingray-42 insulators,'* thought Wilbur. His friend sold the outdated glass fittings as paperweights for three dollars apiece, so he ferreted around in the scrubs along a dirt road hemming the Interstate 75 and picked up a few of the discarded green globes for his pal. Pleased with his haul, Wilbur headed back up the embankment to his truck. And that's when he spotted the bundle: a five-foot long hunk of army green tarpaulin, tied with rope. Curious, Wilbur approached the bizarre parcel. He clawed at the canvas, and it gaped a little, emitting a putrid smell he could taste. Wilbur shuddered, choked, then nudged the bale with the toe of his boot, sending it rolling down the hill. The tarpaulin split wide open, revealing the shape of a human body – a glimpse of flesh, marbled green and purple. Wilbur ran to his truck, then drove two miles to the nearest filling station, where he called Scott County Sheriff, Bobby Vance, from the payphone.

'Bobby Vance arrived with his deputy, Jimmy Williams, and Deputy Coroner Kenneth Grant,' Wilbur told Todd that afternoon, peering over the solid black rims of his glasses. 'I led them to the bundle and, as Bobby bent to examine it, he gagged. Jimmy said, "There's only one odour in the world like that: the stench of rotting human flesh."'

The officers cut the rope ties and peeled open the canvas fully to reveal the naked, putrefied body. The young woman had no eyes, and her right hand was clenched, suggesting she had tried to escape from the tent bag.

Coroner Grant's preliminary autopsy report revealed the victim was a white female aged between sixteen and nineteen; around five foot and one inch tall; with short, red-brown hair; and a noticeable gap between her top front teeth. She had no other identifying marks or scars.

Scott County Attorney Virgil Pryor led a campaign to identify the victim and drafted in top Ohio coroner, Dr Frank Cleveland, to perform an autopsy on her remains. A slight discolouration of the woman's skull indicated a possible head injury, but the coroner could not distinguish her exact cause of death.

Policeman and artist Harold Musser sketched a graphite impression of the nameless woman, working from the autopsy photographs. The image, highlighting the gap between the victim's teeth, featured on flyers which were circulated in town. Local newspapers also printed the drawing – the *Kentucky Post & Times Star* became the first publication to give the victim the name 'Tent Girl'.

Transfixed by the story so far, Todd fired questions at Wilbur: 'What did the police do next?' 'Were any suspects identified?' 'Do you think the victim suffocated inside the tent wrapping?'

Before Todd left the Riddles' home that day, Wilbur showed him a copy of *Master Detective* magazine from May 1969. The issue contained an article titled 'Who is the Tent Girl and Who Killed Her?', chronicling the events on the day Wilbur had found her corpse. Wilbur was cited under a pseudonym in the piece, which also featured Harold Musser's drawing. Wilbur gestured at Tent Girl's face on the yellowing page and gave Todd a solemn look. 'This girl's got a mother. She's got a daddy. She could have a husband. We've got to find out who this girl is,' he said.

Todd nodded slowly. 'I want to help find her,' he said, and he meant every word.

Nine months later, as he'd vowed to his friend in the school cafeteria he would, Todd married Lori. But even in those blissful newlywed days, Todd could not stop thinking about Tent Girl. He'd started researching the story months before he and Lori set up home together in Livingston after they both graduated from high school in the summer of 1998 (Lori left school a year early after passing a General Educational Development test, which certified she had American high school-level academic skills). Todd had spent hours in libraries, hunched inside microfiche booths, eyes scanning through miles of records. Todd went into newspaper offices to view their archived articles about Tent Girl. He tracked down the journalists who wrote those stories, some of whom were long retired, and reread the *Master Detective* feature until he knew it by heart.

Todd passed his daylight hours obsessively hunting for Tent Girl's identity. By night, he worked at a factory that made parts for air-conditioning machines. But Tent Girl would be there with Todd throughout those nocturnal shifts. Her face, as portrayed in Harold Musser's sketch, would come to life in his mind – developing like a Polaroid photograph, gaining colour in her cheeks, and reclaiming her brown eyes. In his mind's eye he would see the gap between her teeth when she smiled. Tent Girl was no longer a spectre to Todd; she was real – living in his head with a merry-go-round of meditations and theories. '*How could a young woman go missing and be killed, and her family not report it to anyone? Surely,* somebody *must know who Tent Girl is? Somebody must miss her. Somebody must have once changed her diaper, fed her and combed her hair. Somebody must have cared for her.*'

Todd's in-laws moved back to Kentucky after the wedding. Lori missed her parents terribly, so, most weekends, the newlyweds would drive 227 miles across the country to visit the Riddles. Todd looked forward to these trips as they meant he could further quiz Wilbur about Tent Girl and visit the site where he had found her decaying body twenty years ago.

Todd would also spend time at Tent Girl's grave that was marked with a sad epitaph. Below the engraving of Musser's sketch, the following facts served as the only known facts of the woman's short life:

TENT GIRL
FOUND MAY 17, 1968
ON U.S. HIGHWAY 25, N
DIED ABOUT APRIL 26–MAY 3, 1968
AGE ABOUT 16–19 YEARS
HEIGHT 5 FEET 1 INCH
WEIGHT 110 TO 115 LBS
REDDISH BROWN HAIR
UNIDENTIFIED

Being at the spot she had been discovered and the place where she rested, fired Todd's determination to find her true identity. Todd remembers the first time Wilbur took him to where he'd stumbled across the canvas bundle. 'It was striking,' he tells me, swaying his head to the rhythm of his words. 'Visiting those locations was important to me. Law enforcement officers have no purpose to go back to a scene when it's dramatically altered after decades. But watching Wilbur retrace his steps, showing me the exact location where he found Tent Girl . . . well, that inspired me. I felt a strong connection to her. I felt I *knew* my Tent Girl. And every time I knelt at her grave and read that tragic last line saying "Unidentified", I would promise her, "I'm going to bring you home. I am going to find your name."'

Investigators had long maintained that Tent Girl was a teenager – possibly as young as thirteen – because she was small. But – based on his conversations with Wilbur and information contained in original police reports – Todd began to question Tent Girl's age. She had well developed breasts, Wilbur recalled, and manicured finger and toenails – which suggested she was unlikely to be a very young teenager. While scanning the FBI's lab report, Todd spotted a clue suggesting a possibility that Tent Girl might be older than the age bracket etched on her headstone. According to the report, a remnant of material found on the victim's shoulder came from a baby's nappy.

Todd says, 'Immediately I thought Tent Girl could be older than suggested – and the nappy found with her led me to think she could be a mother. I wrote to the authorities, explaining my theories. I also wrote to the county coroner and asked for Tent Girl's remains to be exhumed so that her pelvic area could be examined to see whether she'd given birth. I got nowhere with that, but I would keep searching for my Tent Girl.'

As the years slipped by, Todd's fixation on Tent Girl began to spiral out of control. His search for answers put a strain on his marriage. He and Lori would argue over the mounting cost of his research – the thousands of dollars he'd spent on petrol making trips to Kentucky: driving to law enforcement and newspaper offices, to interview residents, reporters, police officers and even the local undertaker who handled Tent Girl's burial. He'd racked up huge phone bills, which they struggled to pay on Todd's minimum wage from the factory. But despite this, Todd could not – and would not – let go of his Tent Girl. She haunted his dreams. One such episode has never left Todd, and hearing this tale today makes me shiver all over.

'I woke up in bed one night, having heard a noise. Creaking footsteps, coming from downstairs in the kitchen,' Todd begins. 'I remember getting out of bed and walking down the stairs and into the kitchen. And there's this figure on the couch, wrapped in canvas. I asked, "Who are you?" And a female voice replied,

"Cut me out and you'll know. Get me out of this bag and I'll tell you who I am."

'So, I opened the kitchen drawer, took out a butcher's knife, and a second or so later, I'm leaning over the figure on the couch. I can feel the vibrations of the blade as I cut through the material until I see this hole, a dark slit in the canvas that suddenly pops open – and this decomposed, eyeless face falls out.'

Todd pauses then, but I want to know, 'What happened next?'

'Oh, I just woke up in bed,' he replies. 'But when I went downstairs in the morning, the butcher's knife was there on the couch. I tried to forget about the nightmare but, I admit, it scared me to think I'd actually taken that knife out of the drawer.'

By 1997, Todd still hadn't identified Tent Girl, but, after saving for a computer, he finally had a dial-up internet connection at home. Yahoo Search – Google had not yet launched – became Todd's new go-to place for information. He combed websites with missing person lists and messages on forums posted by people searching for long-lost friends and relatives. A search for missing carnival workers drew a blank. And there was little information about the case of Tent Girl on the web, Todd observed. He had far more material on the victim in his head and in the hundreds of pages of documents he'd amassed over the years than what was available to some seventy million internet users. *If I digitise all this information, Tent Girl will have a global audience. Surely, somebody must know who Tent Girl is? Somebody must miss her.*' So, Todd created a website dedicated to Tent Girl. 'I published everything I knew about her, along with my beliefs about her possible identity. I included an image of the police sketch and pictures of Tent Girl's grave and the spot where she was found. I sent Tent Girl into cyberspace, hoping that somebody, somewhere, might know who she was.'

Emails trickled into Todd's website inbox. People suggested the names of missing women that might be Tent Girl, but the assiduous sleuth had already eliminated the names.

Then, one night in January 1998, after searching at least four-hundred descriptions of missing women, Todd clicked onto the now defunct Crane & Hibbs web page, an advertisement site like today's Craigslist. It was late, just after midnight and Todd had been online for at least ten hours. His eyelids sagged with tiredness. *'Just one last search and I'll call it a night,'* he thought. In the Crane & Hibbs search engine box, he typed: 'Missing sister Kentucky,' and stabbed the return key. He waited, elbows planted on the desk, jaw heavy in the heels of his hands, watching the hypnotic swirl of the page-loading symbol as it throbbed. *'Why is the internet so slow?'* The monitor gave a lazy grey wink, then flashed its response. Todd's elbows slid east and west as he leaned closer to the screen. He scanned the message once, twice – his heartbeat knocking in his ears. The post, by a woman named Rosemary Westbrook, read: 'My sister Barbara has been missing from our family since the latter part of 1967. She has brown hair, brown eyes, is around five-feet-two, and was last seen in the Lexington, Kentucky area. If you have any information, please contact me at the address posted.'

Todd rocketed from his chair, ran upstairs, burst into the bedroom and snapped on the light. 'Lori, wake up, I've found her. I've found Tent Girl,' he said, jiggling his wife's shoulder. Lori opened her eyes, a sleepy smile playing on her lips. 'I knew you'd find her,' she said. Previous arguments notwithstanding, Lori always admired Todd's tenacity. Throughout the years she had wanted nothing more than for him to find a name for Tent Girl.

Looking back on that moment, Todd admits he 'jumped the gun.' 'I didn't know at that point whether I had found Tent

Girl, but I had this overwhelming feeling of, "*This is it – this is over.*" I tried contacting Rosemary, but my email bounced back initially. So, I looked up her number – she lived in Arkansas – and called her.' Todd later acknowledged that he was wrong to call Rosemary and should have enlisted the help of police to reach out – something that years of amateur sleuthing has taught him is best and safest practice.

Todd's cold call took Rosemary by surprise but, equally, she was keen to hear what he had to say. As the pair exchanged notes, it emerged that Rosemary's sister bore physical similarities to Tent Girl. Barbara – known as Bobbi to close friends and relatives – had a noticeable gap between her front teeth and reddish-brown hair, Rosemary confirmed. She was married to George Earl Taylor, a travelling circus worker. Barbara – maiden name Hackmann – had worked at a restaurant in Lexington, Kentucky. She was twenty-four when she vanished in December 1967. Barbara and George had an infant daughter. Barbara's daughter was now married with children.

Rosemary was just ten when her sister disappeared. Barbara's family had not reported her missing in 1967 because they didn't know she was living in Kentucky at that time. Rosemary said she and Barbara had two other sisters, Jan Daigle and Marie Copeland. It's understood one of Barbara's other sisters later alerted authorities of her disappearance. When the family approached George, he told them his wife had run off with another man.

By the end of their phone call, Todd and Rosemary agreed there were enough similarities between Barbara and Tent Girl to justify further investigation. Rosemary felt certain. 'I think you've found my sister,' Rosemary told Todd.

Authorities were slow to respond to Todd's second request to have Tent Girl's body exhumed for forensic examination. 'I think they thought I was a nutjob,' he says. 'But we kept on pushing and, finally, they agreed to exhume Tent Girl and compare her DNA to Rosemary's.'

The exhumation took place on 2 March, 1998, and Tent Girl's remains were sent to a lab in Frankfort, Kentucky for DNA extraction. This profile would then be compared with a swab provided by Rosemary. Dr Emily Craig, an anthropologist at Scott County's Medical Examiner's Office, immediately concluded that Tent Girl was, in fact, aged between twenty and thirty, but Todd and Rosemary would wait another six weeks for the DNA comparison results.

Towards the end of April 1998, Dr Craig called Todd. She asked if he and Rosemary could attend a press conference the following day at Scott County Courthouse. 'There's going to be an announcement,' she said. 'I can't say what that announcement is, but I wouldn't make you guys drive here for nothing.'

'Sure, I can do that,' said Todd and hung up, feeling dazed. He sat down at his desk, looked up at the framed photograph of Tent Girl's grave on the wall above his computer. The picture had served as his motivation for the last decade. 'Barbara,' he said to the gravestone marked 'unidentified'. 'Your name's Barbara Hackmann Taylor.'

Dr Craig ushered Todd aside when he arrived at the courthouse the next day. He remembers her exact words. 'She immediately grabbed me by the hand and pulled me into a custodian's closet. She said, "You're gonna be the first person to hear this. The Tent Girl is indeed Barbara Hackmann Taylor. Her DNA was a match with Rosemary's. We're gonna go out there and announce this to the world, but you deserve to hear this before everybody else does." And although I was expecting this news, I was still stunned. I must have looked like a ghost when I stepped outside. I didn't know what to say. There was a media crowd and Rosemary and her other sisters were there, and I saw both joy and sadness on their faces. I couldn't believe it was finally over.'

Barbara's family chose to rebury her in the same Georgetown Cemetery where she had lain unidentified for thirty years. Beneath the original 'Tent Girl' marker they placed an additional stone, bearing her nickname, 'Bobbie' and the inscription, 'Loving Mother, Grandmother & Sister.'

Family and friends of Barbara described her husband, George Taylor, as a violent man. Police believed he had struck Barbara on the head during an argument, knocking her unconscious, then wrapped and tied her in the tarpaulin before dumping her at the roadside. Barbara was left to suffocate inside her tent prison. Officers later tried to find Taylor, only to learn he'd died of cancer in 1987.

Discovering Tent Girl's identity was what turned Todd into a celebrity. Media organisations clamoured to interview the man they'd dubbed 'the world's first internet sleuth'. Todd appeared on CBS's true crime documentary *48 Hours*, and NBC's Leeza Gibbons' talk show, *Leeza,* as well as multiple other television shows and documentaries. One of his proudest moments, however, came in 2001 when *Master Detective* magazine published a feature he wrote about his ten-year campaign to connect Tent Girl with a name. The piece, 'The Thirty-year Mystery of the Tent Girl', merged the original article by the late Alan Marksfield with Todd's prose to conclude the story. This time, Wilbur was happy to be named. He remembered his words to Todd eleven years ago: 'We've got to find out who this girl is,' and he recalled the meaningful look on Todd's face when he promised to do just that. Wilbur was bursting with pride for his son-in-law and acknowledged his dogged efforts in the *Master Detective* sequel. 'Todd has put in more than a thousand hours on this case. There's no law enforcement office that worked harder on any case than Todd did on this one.' Wilbur passed away in 2017, aged ninety, but his story of how he found the woman in the circus tent bag lives on. 'Wilbur was proud of his story – and it was *his* story. He found Barbara.'

Todd slopes off screen for a second, then returns holding a turquoise glass globe. It's a Hemingray-42 insulator. Todd has a family of them, he says, who live on the shelf in his Doe office, keeping company with clay Sally. He holds the insulator up to the camera, twisting it slightly. It looks like a glass snowman, scarved and hatted, but its purpose long ago was to aid telephone communication by insulating signals. 'Whenever I look at these insulators I think of Wilbur. The telephone wires went over the patch where he found Barbara. And it was through telephone lines [the dial-up internet] that we managed to give her back her name. This is very symbolic to me.'

Todd and Rosemary are good friends today and they regularly speak on the phone or meet up when their paths cross. Both are devoted to keeping Barbara's memory alive.

I suggest to Todd that Tent Girl's grave could still read 'unidentified' were it not for his sedulous efforts. He can't be sure of that, he says, adding, 'It was a miracle to find Rosemary's message. One minute less looking, and I may never have found her. Ultimately, there might have been enough data out there one day, and the case might have eventually come together. But equally, it might have been something that passed in the night, never to be realised again.' Although, Todd admits, Tent Girl will always be his 'baby'.

Nowadays, Todd runs an online fashion business with Lori while also working as a substitute teacher at his former high school, Livingston Academy, where he met his wife *and* Tent Girl. Each time he enters the school building he's transported back to 1987. 'I feel like a ghost wandering the corridors,' he tells me. But Todd's true passion for identifying decedents and providing answers for their relatives is palpable and still takes up a lot of his free time. So far, the Doe Network has identified over a hundred Does and has gathered data to keep thousands of similar cases in the public eye. Todd receives several emails and calls every week from families hoping to trace their missing loved ones – and he goes above and beyond to help every one of them. As he attests: 'Sadly, we can't bring a Doe back, but we can bring them home to their families and give them a name.'

3

My First 'Solve'

Citizen sleuth Ellen Leach is best known for identifying a human skull found in a bucket of cement at a Missouri truck stop – a match she made on her clunky computer some eight hundred miles away from where the decayed head was discovered.

One evening in 2004, after clocking off from her day job running the seasonal department at a branch of Hobby Lobby, a popular US arts and crafts chain store, Ellen drove to her home in Gulfport, Mississippi. There, after getting stuck into her quotidian post-work chores: the dishes, laundry, making dinner – 'all that stuff that needs to be done,' as Ellen puts it – she settled in front of her computer to pursue her nightly passion: combing the internet for clues that might match unidentified bodies to missing person cases.

That night, Ellen found herself returning to a picture recently uploaded to the Doe Network (International Center for Unidentified and Missing Persons) website's list of unidentified people. The image showed forensic sculptor Jack Bender's reconstruction of a head that belonged to a man in his fifties who had been murdered. The victim was white, with receding grey-sandy hair. He had a long nose – straight bridge but bulbous around the nostrils with a slightly hooked tip. His eyebrows, dense, charcoal and hawkish over his greeny-grey eyes. Fleshy jawline and lips. The image was an incredible work of art that communicated a grisly backstory which had confounded detectives for the last three years. It was a story that had been on Ellen's radar well before Bender's reconstruction emerged.

In April 2001, retired haulier Ronald Telfer spotted an abandoned bucket filled with hardened cement at Kearney Truck Plaza, Missouri. The vessel would be handy for feeding his pigs at home, he thought. Emptying its contents, he was assailed by a putrid smell as the concrete thumped onto the ground, but he left with the bucket assuming the mass he was leaving behind contained animal remains.

Four months later, builder Franklin Dean noticed the discarded concrete cylinder at the same truck stop. 'The cement was blocking Franklin's way as he went to park up,' Ellen tells me during our conversation via video call. 'So, he leapt out of his truck and tried to move the obstruction. As he did this, he spotted what looked like a human skull and hair poking through the concrete. Turned out, it *was* a human skull. But police had no idea who the victim was – and at that point, no further remains had been found.

'This case intrigued me from the beginning. Even back then I wanted to solve the case. It was a hard one, for sure. It was a challenging investigation for police because, initially, they had no reconstruction of the skull. But then the police department came out with Frank Bender's imitation of the victim – and he looked familiar. I had seen this guy before on a missing person's website, but I couldn't think which one or where he was from. So, I had to go back through my files and, God knows how many missing persons sites, to find his picture.'

Ellen's lilting Southern accent doesn't seem to fit the macabre tale she recounts of a cement-encased head. I feel she should instead be talking about the apple pies that 'Momma used to bake.' But her dedication shines through as she goes on to document her relentless search for the man portrayed in Bender's bust. She sifted through thousands of names of men who'd gone missing from all corners of America until, finally, the face she had recalled reappeared on her screen.

His name was Greg May, a fifty-five-year-old tattoo artist and antiques dealer who vanished from his home in Bellevue – an intricate jigsaw piece Iowan city girdled by the Mississippi River.

'As soon as I saw Greg May's picture, I remembered him,' says Ellen. 'This was a case I'd returned to several times in the last year. His disappearance wasn't listed on the Doe Network. Instead, I'd found Greg on Iowa's Missing Person Information Clearing House website. Greg seemed like a decent guy, somebody I wanted to find.'

Comparing Greg May's photograph to Bender's reconstruction, Ellen was struck by the facial similarities right away. Although the image of Greg was in black and white, his eyebrows were noticeably darker than his hair. They were thick brows too, like those on the bust. 'The only obvious difference was that Greg May had a moustache in this picture. But, looking at his features, they were almost identical. Greg had a strikingly similar jawline, chin and nose to the reconstruction. And, at fifty-five, Greg was the right age, too.'

Firmly believing the man depicted in the clay sculpture could be Greg May, Ellen emailed her information to the Doe Network, who would then need to approve her theory before alerting law enforcement investigators. 'Well,' explains Ellen, leaning back in her chair, 'the Doe Network *did* send my match to law enforcement officials, but the police department was experiencing computer problems, so they didn't receive the information straight away. The whole process got delayed and, meanwhile, I was reading about developments regarding Greg's disappearance in Iowa.'

Divorcee Greg May was reported missing in February 2001 by his son and daughter, Don and Shannon May, who had settled in California. They would contact Greg several times a month for a catch-up but panicked when their calls began to go unanswered.

Greg had moved to Bellevue from Wisconsin a year earlier to embrace a Mark Twain-style life on the banks of the Mississippi. Described as 'distinguished' and 'polite', Greg had a sharp eye for Civil War relics, and his burgeoning collection of artefacts, including guns, uniforms and documents, was worth tens of thousands of dollars at the time he went missing.

In Bellevue, the tattooist shared a rented house with his lifelong friend Douglas DeBruin, an ex-con known by his nickname, 'Moose', who cut an imposing figure with his hulking inked limbs. The pair usually breakfasted together at Bellevue's Frontier Café. At night they necked beers over games of pool in bars lining N. Riverview Drive. The friends even worked together at a tattoo parlour across the river in Illinois. At weekends, DeBruin helped Greg buy and sell war antiques. Back then, things were going well for Greg. He'd met an attractive Illinois woman, Jan Buman, with whom he planned to retire to Florida. But things soon changed after DeBruin's girlfriend, Julie Miller, moved in with the two men.

One evening in January 2001, Jan arrived at Greg's house. Greg had invited her over to discuss their move to Florida. He said he'd leave the back door open. But Jan found the back door locked. She knocked several times and when no one answered she grew concerned. The house was silent, its windows shuttered, but there was a small gap between broken slats covering one pane. Peering through that hole, Jan noticed Greg's feet. He appeared to be sitting down but didn't react when she called his name and banged her fist against the glass. Panicking, Jan hurried to a nearby restaurant to dial Greg's number. The line went directly to voicemail, so Jan called Greg's landlord, who refused to let her into the property. With her options to reach Greg seemingly exhausted, Jan drove home.

When two days passed with no word from Greg, Jan assumed he'd had a change of heart about their relationship. A call from Julie Miller confirmed her theory. 'Greg's asked me to tell you that he doesn't want to see you anymore,' she said. 'Oh, and he's moving to Florida without you.' Jan was mortified, thinking, *'At least he could have had the decency to tell me himself.'*

A few weeks later, Don and Shannon travelled to Iowa, after failing to reach their father by phone. They were both hoping to discover that their dad had simply taken off for a while, as he often did, to hunt antiques. But they arrived in Bellevue to a deserted house. There was no sign of Greg or his cherished war antiques, and the landline had been disconnected. DeBruin and his girlfriend were nowhere to be seen, either.

Desperate for answers, the siblings contacted Jan, who told them about the night she'd seen Greg's unmoving feet through the window and the subsequent call from Miller. 'He's apparently moved to Florida,' said Jan, but Don and Shannon knew this couldn't be true. Their dad was a spontaneous man, granted, but, as Don pointed out, 'We're a close family. He wouldn't just move without telling us.' Fearing the worst, Don called Bellevue Police. 'Our dad is missing,' he choked out to the officer.

By the end of February, a major search operation was underway, but the residents of Bellevue offered police little information about Greg or his housemates. Some had never even heard of Greg. His landlord, however, said DeBruin had contacted him on New Year's Day to say he and Greg were ending their lease and moving away. DeBruin was then seen loading Greg's entire antiques collection into a yellow van before driving off with Miller, the landlord claimed.

Don and Shannon continued to search for their dad. They offered a $15,000 reward for information leading to Greg's whereabouts and flooded the area with leaflets. A breakthrough finally happened in the spring when investigators found the missing man's car in a parking lot in Illinois. Greg's wallet was inside the vehicle.

Then, Don received an alarming phone call from a friend of his dad, saying he'd spotted some of Greg's war antiques featured in an Illinois auction house catalogue. The items, including confederate swords and Civil War uniforms, had been put up for auction by Julie Miller. This tip led officers in a new direction when the Illinois auctioneers confirmed that Julie Miller and DeBruin were en route to Flagstaff, Arizona to sell more of Greg's prized treasures. In April, the pair were finally caught in the Grand Canyon state. They were arrested on theft charges. DeBruin and Miller insisted they owned the antiques. 'They're ours, we can sell 'em if we want,' moaned DeBruin. When later asked about Greg's whereabouts, he lifted his tattooed shoulders and told investigators, 'Last time I heard about him he was heading out to Illinois.'

Under questioning, Miller painted a disturbingly different picture. 'He's dead,' she announced. 'It was an accident. He [Greg] and Moose had a fist fight and Greg died. I have no idea what Moose did with Greg's body.'

Investigators did not buy Miller's fist-fight tale; they knew Greg's death was no accident. DeBruin had murdered Greg out of sheer greed – for the quarter of a million-dollar war collection he'd helped his friend amass over the last thirty years. Proving this, however, would not be easy. Aside from a small trace of Greg's blood on DeBruin's jacket, prosecutors had little else to work with. Murder convictions in the absence of remains or other physical evidence of killing are rare – and DeBruin's case would be the first murder trial without a body in Iowa. So, the prosecution struck a deal with Miller, promising her immunity if she testified against DeBruin. Miller agreed – and subsequently pleaded guilty to theft and the transportation of stolen property over state lines. She was jailed for three years in March 2004, but she claimed she knew nothing about the whereabouts of Greg's body.

DeBruin was charged with his friend's murder and his trial was set for April 2005, but as that date approached, Greg's body had still not been found. Prosecutor John Kies had no proof of Greg's death and would therefore need to rely on circumstantial evidence and Miller's testimony to get a conviction.

Just two days before DeBruin was due to appear in the dock, Ellen Leach received a call from Traycie Sherwood, a fellow Doe Network volunteer. Traycie had finally heard back from Sergeant Tom O'Leary, the detective leading the skull-in-a-bucket case for Kearney Police Department. He confirmed that the head had been identified through dental records.

It was a moment Ellen will never forget. 'I was at home when I got the call,' she says. 'And, you know, I had been chasing this case for months, waiting to hear whether my match was correct. Then Traycie told me, "You were right, Ellen. The head belongs to Greg May."'

The identification came just in time for Kies, who now had physical evidence to prove that DeBruin murdered Greg. Police also faced the harrowing task of breaking the news to Don and Shannon. The siblings were heartbroken but relieved they could now lay their dad to rest and, hopefully, see justice served. Don told reporters at the time: 'I had almost resigned myself to never finding Dad's remains. The timing is fortuitous . . . it was about to be the first trial without a body.' Don and Shannon contacted Ellen; they thanked her profusely – and promptly paid her the $15,000 reward money.

Matching the head found in a bucket of cement to Greg May was Ellen's 'first solve', she tells me. And I must say, I'm hugely impressed. Ellen's eagle-eyed detective work had not only brought closure to a grieving family but had significantly changed the landscape of a murder trial. 'This case was to be the first in Iowa to be trialled without a body, but I brought the body to them. And while I was pleased about this, I also felt so sad for Don and Shannon for having to go through such trauma,' she says.

The horrific details of Greg's murder were laid bare by Miller when she stepped into the witness box at DeBruin's trial. DeBruin strangled Greg with a yellow nylon cord in the house the trio shared in Bellevue, she told the court. Miller went on to explain how she then helped DeBruin move Greg's lifeless body to the basement, where the pair dismembered the corpse. DeBruin heaved Greg onto a washing machine – then hacked off his head and limbs with a chainsaw while Miller used a kitchen knife to butcher other body parts. The next day, Miller watched as DeBruin placed Greg's severed head into a bucket of wet cement. She helped pack Greg's mutilated limbs into bin bags which they loaded into the back of DeBruin's Volvo. The jury heard how the evil duo tossed those bags, one by one, into ravines as they drove twenty miles northwest to Dubuque, Iowa. Here, they dumped the chainsaw and some of Greg's clothing at a goodwill collection site.

Miller further testified that she then drove Greg's car to Illinois. The couple returned to the Bellevue murder scene to pick up the bucket containing Greg's encased head, which they placed in the back of the yellow van with the dead man's antique collection. They drove for almost four hundred miles then stopped overnight at Kearney Truck Plaza, Missouri. The following morning, DeBruin ditched the five-gallon vessel holding the head of his friend at the truck stop.

The jury in DeBruin's murder trial deliberated for less than an hour before returning a guilty verdict. Convicted of first-degree murder and first-degree theft, DeBruin was jailed for life without parole in May 2005. The killer was handed a further ten years for the theft, with the sentences to run consecutively.

Following Miller's vivid testimony, she pleaded guilty to a federal perjury charge, which landed her a five-year prison sentence in March 2006. She was never charged with Greg's murder because of the deal she struck with investigators.

Although unbearable for Don and Shannon to process, Miller's shocking admission did provide clues as to where to look for the rest of their dad's remains. Volunteers joined them as they scoured vertiginous woodland slopes hemming US Highway 52 (US 52). While rifling through a grim carpet of animal carcasses and strewn rubbish, Don found what appeared to be a severed human bone. Forensic experts concluded the fragment was indeed a right femur that had probably been 'cut with a saw blade.'

The thought of their father being 'discarded like trash' shattered the siblings' hearts. Shannon said shortly after their nightmare discovery: 'This is where people put their trash. My father wasn't trash. He was a human being. Part of this makes me really angry – because I know there are remains out there that will never be found.'

DeBruin's life sentence, while welcomed by Don and Shannon, would never mitigate their life sentence of heartache caused by the absence of their father. But there was one person to whom they'd remain ever thankful: Ellen Leach. The three kept in touch with regular emails and phone calls and would exchange Christmas cards every year. Ellen informs me that

Don passed away in 2021 although she tells me, 'I still speak with Shannon – I'll always stay in touch with her.'

The Greg May case would be the first of many 'solves' for Ellen, who's earned a stellar reputation for being one of the best cyber gumshoes in America. When I ask what inspires her drive to give names to lost loved ones, Ellen's eyes darken and her shoulders sag as she exhales at length. There's a pause, and then she begins to speak again.

'Well, ma'am, in 1994, my cousin's wife killed their babies. Two little boys – Michael, who was three, and Alexander . . . he was just fourteen months when it happened. But my cousin's wife lied. She went on national television and cried, saying a black man had stolen her car and her babies.'

The story Ellen tells me made international headlines when it broke. Susan Smith, then married to Ellen's cousin David, claimed a black man carjacked her in South Carolina and sped away with their two boys still in the back seat. A November 1994 newsclip captures a twenty-three-year-old Susan, sobbing as she sends a seemingly poignant message to her 'missing' children. 'I wanna say, to my babies, that Momma loves you very much,' she weeps. 'You guys have got to be strong – because I just feel in my heart that you're OK.'

'Well,' says Ellen, 'turned out there was no carjacking. Susan took the boys out in the car and drove them to Lake John D. Long near Union, South Carolina. Then, with Michael and Alexander strapped in the back seat, she put the car into drive mode, jumped out and watched the vehicle roll into the lake. The boys drowned.'

Smith was eventually convicted of the killings in 1995 and will be eligible for parole in 2024. 'Before it emerged that Susan had killed the boys, we thought they were missing. So, I started searching missing person indexes. I was trying to find Michael and Alexander and get some sense of what was going on. As I searched, I noticed there were so many missing people out there who needed help. And that's what inspired me to search other cases. I wanted to help bring closure for the families – so they're not sitting at home for forty years wondering when their loved ones will come home.'

According to NamUs database, more than 600,000 people go missing, and approximately 4,400 unidentified bodies are recovered in the United States every year. Ellen works alone and focusses on the 'less talked about' and most challenging cold cases. She is methodical and relentless in her approach, which has led to her identifying eight people. 'I'll only work on one case at a time, but once I start digging, I'll dig for days, weeks or months until I find something I think is a match. I start by going through the unidentified lists until I find a case that I think I can solve. I try to find cases I know other amateur sleuths might avoid, such as the skull in the bucket scenario. Many online detectives will try to solve the whole-body cases, whereas I look at the body parts ones.'

Geography and distance are key factors when connecting an unidentified body to a missing person, Ellen maintains. She describes how she helped match remains found in a canal to missing Floridian, Robert Ezell in 2005. 'This time, there was only a police composite drawing available of Robert, who went missing in Jacksonville. The unidentified body was found in November 2001, around the time Robert Ezell went missing. In this case, the unidentified remains were found just twenty miles away from where Robert Ezell disappeared, so I put two and two together and suggested a match based on distance. And it turned out I was right. Police were able to identify the remains found in the canal to Robert Ezell through fingerprints.'

Distance was again a pointer during Ellen's next investigation in November 2007. Returning to the Doe Network's gallery of the 'unidentified', the sleuth was drawn to a post about remains of a young woman found in Florida. Searching the Florida Unidentified Decedents Database (FLUIDDB), Ellen found a report on the case. There were no composite images available, but the file did state that the skeletal remains were found in a remote field at 6001 W. 28 Avenue, Hialeah, Florida, on 20 April, 1981. The report said the deceased woman was white, between eleven and twenty years old, and around five foot six, with 'fairly long hair in a ponytail'. When found, she was wearing a 'white blouse with blue squared design stripes' and 'Derrieres brand blue jeans'. Dental information confirmed the victim had an overbite.

'The overbite caught my eye,' notes Ellen. 'So, I started going through the missing persons lists, looking for any young women who'd vanished in the Florida region and that's when I discovered Jean Marie Stewart.'

Jean Marie Stewart was sixteen when she vanished in Cypress Village, Miami Lakes, less than five miles from where the remains were found in Hialeah. She was last seen with her boyfriend on the evening of 25 March, 1980. That night, the couple had stopped at a 7-Eleven store as they drove home from a party. Jean's boyfriend went into the shop, but when he returned to the car minutes later, Jean was nowhere to be seen. She'd left her purse, shoes and money inside the vehicle. The missing person appeal for Jean said she was wearing jeans and a shirt at the time of her disappearance. 'She has protruding upper front teeth,' the post concluded.

'When I read the post, I immediately thought the body found in Hialeah must be Jean Marie Stewart,' Ellen recalls. 'First, the distance between Cypress Village and the field in Hialeah was just a few miles or so. Secondly, Jean was within the age range specified in the FLUIDDB report, and she was wearing jeans – as was the victim. But it was the "protruding upper front teeth" that really struck me. Jean had an overbite. I thought, *"I hope they have dental records for her."'*

Ellen faxed her theory to Miami-Dade Police. 'Detective Robert called me within the hour. She was excited about the possible match and said she was gonna get it checked out.' Two weeks later, she called Ellen. 'I'm elated,' Robert gushed. 'We found Jean Marie Stewart's dental records and the Miami Dade County medical examiner has confirmed they match the Hialeah remains. Jean Marie Stewart has been positively identified. Congratulations, Ellen.'

After twenty-seven agonising years, Jean Marie's parents could finally lay their daughter to rest. She was buried in her home city of Pittsburgh, Pennsylvania in 2008. Around that time, news outlets in Pittsburgh reported that Hialeah Police Department had launched a homicide investigation into Jean Marie's death, but there have been no further updates on the investigation since.

'I don't know whether Jean Marie's parents will ever find out what happened to her, but it made me feel happy to know that I helped to bring their girl home,' says Ellen.

Her growing portfolio of 'solves' also includes matching a jawbone to a runaway woman three years after she went missing and identifying a male suicide victim by his boots. 'Often, the answer to the puzzle is in the overlooked details. The unidentified suicide victim was found in woods in Maine. He had on DeWalt boots, so I did some research, figuring the Doe might have worked in a store that sold these boots – people working in stores will wear that store's clothing because they get a staff discount, right? Anyway, I found that Sears sold DeWalt boots – and I also discovered a young missing man from Pennsylvania, Kevin O'Brien, who used to work at a Sears store.

'I submitted my information to the chief medical examiner in Maine, naming Kevin O'Brien [as a potential identification for the body]. This one took a while to come back – a little over a year – but the examiner said DNA tests had confirmed my match. That was a fairly easy one to solve, but oddly a long-distance case as Kevin was found 447 miles away from his home city.'

Law enforcement is not always welcoming of citizen detectives, and Ellen attests she has encountered her fair share of bristly officials who 'don't listen to me.' But equally, she has cultivated a good number of trusted contacts across America. Some detectives share case files with the Mississippi sleuth and, occasionally, coroners hand photographs of victims to her. 'Whenever I put in a match for an unidentified, I get varied responses from law enforcement departments. Some are dismissive, sure; they don't take me seriously. To them, I'm just an everyday Joe. Others are real responsive though – and thankful, too.

'Coroners generally don't like to give out their information, but two have done so for me. Those cases – in Virginia and Wisconsin – didn't work out. Not all cases work out – and I only submit matches I'm confident about. I never post my thoughts online before a match has been confirmed. I just pass my information to law enforcement and let them decide.'

Ellen makes her 'matches' sound like easy work, but she assures me this is not the case and offers some sage advice to wannabe home detectives. 'You have got to be patient. You're not gonna make a match overnight. I know people who have worked for years without a positive result. It took me five years before I made a match – and then they happened one after the other.'

But what's next for the woman who gave a name to the head in a bucket? Ellen's currently working on two cases, the first of which she's already submitted a likely match for. 'I can't name names as I wouldn't want to give false hope to the victim's family.

However, this case is a young man who went missing from Mississippi. I think I've matched him to unidentified remains found in Alabama. But I'm waiting on the DNA results, which could take several months.'

The second mystery, says Ellen, is one of an unidentified homeless man found dead in Florida. 'The strange thing about this one is that the victim was supposedly homeless – yet he had thousands of dollars in cash in his pocket when his body was found. So, I don't think he was homeless. I think this was somebody who was running from the law.' This sounds like a needle in a haystack task to me. There are hundreds of fugitives listed on the FBI's website, I tell her. 'Yeah, I'm still trying to find the Florida one,' admits Ellen. Then she inches her face closer to the camera and her eyebrows flit to her pewter hairline. 'It's proving a little difficult, but I will find him. Yes, ma'am, I will find him.'

I'm sure she will.

4

Websleuths

Murray, Utah, September 1974

Tucking her long, hazelnut hair behind her ears Tricia Griffith sashayed through Sears in Fashion Place shopping mall with a newfound confidence. She had on a cornflower-print shirt, knotted at her midriff and flared jeans that swished to the beat of Lynyrd Skynyrd's song 'Sweet Home Alabama' that ran through her mind. The track had blared from the stereo when her big brother, Craig, had dropped her off at the mall in his Gremlin a few minutes ago. Now Tricia couldn't get the jerky rhythm out of her head.

As she wended her way through racks displaying back-to-school clothes, Tricia glimpsed her reflection in a wall mirror. A svelte-yet-curvy figure filled the glass. She looked pretty hip in her outfit and lip-gloss, she thought, her hair parted in the middle – the *de rigueur* look of the moment. Tricia had just turned fifteen, but she felt every inch a woman. Today's shopping spree was a big deal for Tricia because this was her first solo trip to the mall and she had thirty dollars in her purse to spend on new school clothes.

It was early evening – a weeknight – and, as usual, the mall was busy. Young kids with their parents, also shopping for school clothes ahead of the fall semester, and the regular clusters of high school students. Fashion Place, with its trendy shops and a movie theatre that stayed open until midnight, was a magnet for teenagers.

'Oh, I was so excited,' says Tricia as we talk online today. 'I was a sophomore – my first year in high school and, for the first time, I was going to the mall by myself. My mother usually went with me.

'My brother Craig drove me to the mall and we'd listened to our radio station. I thought it was so cool. Craig dropped me off and I went straight into Sears, feeling all grown-up. I had a little lip-gloss on, and Mom had given me thirty dollars to get new school clothes. I was thinking about what to buy and daydreaming about getting a boyfriend, but then, argh . . .' Tricia's hands fly to her temples. 'Oh, my stomach flips when I remember what happened next.'

The man seemed to appear from nowhere, but Tricia was instantly struck by his handsomeness. The man was in his late twenties, around six feet tall, with soft brown collar-length hair and sharp, beady eyes of mouthwash blue. His tan trousers and shirt matched his smooth complexion. 'A Cary Grant lookalike,' she thought. He strode up to Tricia, greeted her with a charismatic smile and an over-familiar nod, and, for a moment, teenage Tricia couldn't speak for admiring the view. 'Hey, how are you?' he said, falling into step with Tricia and flashing her another smile that sent her heart aflutter.

'He was perfect. I thought, "Maybe he's in the army?" – because he was head-to-toe in tan and I'd seen soldiers wearing similar clothes,' Tricia recalls. 'He had on smart, dark brown dress shoes. I just remember his hair was perfect, his face was perfect, and that smile . . . I thought it was a gorgeous smile. He had his hands in his trouser pockets as he spoke. He was just so charming, and I was boy-crazy at the time. Oh my God, yeah, I wanted a boyfriend, and he was *so* cute.'

The man asked her for directions to the department store ZCMI – a shop that didn't exist in the Fashion Place mall at that time.

'I looked up at him – he didn't give his name – and said, "Oh my gosh, you're in the wrong mall. There's no ZCMI here. That store's in Cottonwood Mall, which is, like, a few miles ride east from here." And I remember he went, "Aah," and threw his head back with a chuckle. And all this time we're walking side by side, into the mall, and I'm still thinking how handsome he is. I was looking up at him thinking, *"You're adorable."* I wanted him to ask me out on a date.'

Tricia laughed with the stranger. After all, coming to the wrong mall was an easy mistake to make, right? But alarm bells sounded when he then asked her, 'Please, would you come with me and show me how to get to Cottonwood? I have a car. You could come with me, point me in the right direction.' Tricia closes her eyes and shudders, shaking her head as though to rid the memory from her mind.

'For some reason, when he asked me to go with him, I panicked. My blood ran cold and I had this horrible feeling in my stomach. I put my head down and said, "I can't, I can't." But he wouldn't take no for an answer. At this point he's still walking alongside me through the mall, and I'm feeling his intense eyes on me, even though my head is bent. "Oh, come on, just come to the parking lot with me," he insisted, "just point me in the right direction." This didn't feel right at all and I'm like, "No, no, I can't come with you." He asked again, "Please come with me. Show me the way." His tone changed quite suddenly. He sounded panicky – desperate almost.'

Serendipity rescued Tricia from the handsome man who was 'beginning to creep [her] out' when she spotted her cousin, Gerry, coming out of Susie's Casuals shop some ten metres ahead.

'I looked up and spotted Gerry – she was old enough to be my mother. I waved at her and blurted, "There's my mom," then I ran right over to her and said, "Oh my God, Gerry, there was this guy," and I turned to point him out, but he wasn't there. Poof, he'd taken off.

'I went to the payphone and called Craig and told him to pick me up. I said, "I don't want to be here. There is this weird guy." In a heartbeat I'd gone from feeling on top of the world to terrified. Craig, being the protective big brother that he is, turned up with a hammer on the passenger seat of his car. He said, "Let's go find this son of a bitch." I told him, "No. I don't want you to beat him up. The guy was just creepy. It was scary, that's all."'

Tricia would later realise that the handsome man who'd approached her in Fashion Place was the serial killer, Ted Bundy.

* * *

By late October, 1974, Theodore (Ted) Robert Bundy, a twenty-nine-year-old student at University of Utah Law School in Salt Lake City, had killed at least eleven young women – nine in Washington County, Oregon and two known victims in Utah. The predator was known to travel vast distances and across state lines to rape and kill women. He'd dispose of their bodies in remote, mountainous spots – then revisit their decaying corpses to have sex with them.

A month after Tricia's terrifying encounter at the mall, Bundy struck again. His victim was seventeen-year-old Laura

Ann Aime. On 31 October, Bundy kidnapped Laura after she left a Halloween party in Lehi, Utah. He raped and killed her then dumped her naked body. Two hikers found her remains on the side of an embankment in Utah's American Fork Canyon, a month later.

Then, on 8 November, 1974, Bundy prowled the same mall where he'd previously targeted Tricia. Like Tricia, Carol DaRonch, a shy eighteen-year-old, was shopping alone that day when Bundy approached her. Posing as Police Officer Roseland, he cornered Carol as she exited Waldon Book Stores and warned her that somebody had attempted to steal her car. 'What's your registration plate number?' he asked. 'You'll need to file a police report.'

Bundy was not in uniform, but Carol accompanied the seemingly genuine officer to the car park. Her maroon Chevrolet was in the same space in which she'd earlier parked it and seemed untouched. Bundy asked her to accompany him to the local police headquarters to make the report. He then led her to his car – a rundown beige VW Beetle. 'Climb in,' he said with a smile that revealed a row of white teeth.

Carol hesitated and asked Bundy for identification. 'Sure,' he said, still smiling as he flipped open his wallet and flashed what appeared to be a genuine police badge. Assuming Bundy must be undercover or off-duty, Carol got into his car but, as they drove off, she became increasingly nervous. The road on which they were travelling did not lead to the police station. Her driver smelled of alcohol, Carol noticed. And where had his genial smile gone? Now the police officer was shooting her sly sideways looks.

Minutes later, Bundy swerved his car to a halt by a kerb outside an elementary school. Carol panicked and reached for the passenger door handle, but found that there wasn't one. Next, cold metal gripped her left wrist as the man handcuffed her. He pulled out a gun. 'I'll blow your head off,' he sneered.

Carol fought back and scratched and struck her attacker before managing to force open the passenger door. She bolted from the car, screaming for help – for her life – as Bundy chased her, now wielding a crowbar. He gained on her, lifted high the weapon then attempted to smash it down on her head. Fortunately, after a violent struggle, Carol broke free again. She staggered into the snow-banked road, into the path of an oncoming car. She began waving frantically. The vehicle stopped and Carol jumped in. 'Please, take me to the police station,' she told the driver.

Later that same day Bundy, enraged that Carol had escaped, went on to abduct and kill seventeen-year-old Debra Kent.

Bundy's attack on Carol was of special interest to Utah police, who were investigating the disappearance of several young women at that time. Simultaneously, authorities in Seattle were hunting a 'young man called Ted' – a suspect in many murders in the state.

Bundy was finally arrested and charged with Carol's kidnapping after she identified him in a police line-up. She eventually testified against Bundy, who was convicted of aggravated kidnapping and assault in March 1976 and jailed for one to fifteen years.

Tricia recalls reading about Carol's kidnapping in 1975 but Bundy had a chameleon-like ability to change his appearance, and she did not recognise him in the newspaper photo as the man who'd approached her at the Fashion Place mall. The 1975 mugshot revealed a man with a bloated-face; scruffy, chin-length hair; and a coarse beard. It was a far cry from the clean-shaven, immaculate character who'd tried to lure her into his car.

'When I read about Carol DaRonch's ordeal, it did remind me of my own experience – purely because she'd also been targeted at Fashion Place mall. But I honestly didn't recognise Ted Bundy's picture. His face looked all puffy and he had a five-day beard. I never made the connection then, and life carried on. I was a teenager.'

Only two years later, when Tricia read another article in the *Salt Lake Tribune*, did she recognise Bundy. He had made headline news following his escape from Aspen's Pitkin County Courthouse, where he was standing trial for the 1975 slaying of twenty-three-year-old nurse Caryn Campbell. Bundy was representing himself at the trial and had therefore been allowed access to the court's legal library, unshackled. While the court listened to a proposed death penalty motion for Bundy, he had leapt out of the window and sprinted off into the mountains.

'I'll never forget the moment I saw his face again,' Tricia recalls. 'I came downstairs and my dad and brother were reading the newspaper. I looked at the front page and my blood turned to ice. I clapped my hand to my mouth. There he was – the man who'd tried to get me to take a ride with him – staring straight at me with those penetrating eyes. The headline was something like "The Seven Faces of Ted Bundy". There were several pictures of Bundy, illustrating how he changed his looks to evade capture. He was on the run in Colorado at the time. I picked him out from the row of pictures before I read the headline. His face was unmistakeable. He was clean cut and good looking. Pointing at the picture, I called out to my brother. I said, "Oh my God, Craig, that's the guy from Fashion Place mall – the one you wanted to go after with a hammer."'

Assimilating the changing faces of Ted Bundy with the one she remembered, an overwhelming cocktail of emotions churned in Tricia's chest. Her head whirled with questions – 'What if . . . ?' and 'If only . . .' She began to wonder why she hadn't reported her mall incident to police at the time. 'You should've let me go after him,' Craig had said to her, voicing another of his sister's thoughts.

'When I read that article, I realised how I could easily have become another victim of Bundy,' Tricia explains. 'If he had asked me first to go to the parking lot and point him in the right direction, I would have done that. I *absolutely* would have done that. But it was him asking me to take a ride with him that scared me. I panicked.

'Oh, just thinking about that now is making my stomach flip again. Looking back, I was the poster child for a Ted Bundy victim. I weighed a hundred and ten pounds, and my hair was long and parted in the middle – I looked very similar to many of the young women Bundy killed.'

Tricia called an individual named in the 'Seven Faces' article to report her Bundy encounter. 'I can't remember his name, but he was either a police officer or a prosecutor – somebody official. Anyway, I found his number and called him. I said, "I can place Ted Bundy at the Fashion Place mall before he abducted Carol DaRonch – he came after me there, too. In September 1974." I described the man who'd accosted me at the mall – his voice, features and clothes – and explained how he'd wanted me to take a ride with him. I finished by telling him, "I was so sacred, and now I feel so guilty for not reporting him."

'The guy sighed down the phone, then said, "Yeah, that's our Ted. You had a lucky escape there."'

Consumed with guilt for not reporting her encounter with the killer at the mall sooner, Tricia hung-up the phone and read the article once more. The report said Bundy had been wearing tan clothes – a turtleneck jumper, tan corduroy trousers and brown loafers – when he'd jumped from the second-storey library window. '*A similar outfit to that worn by the man who accosted me at the mall,*' thought Tricia.

From that moment, Tricia incessantly followed the Bundy story. She celebrated his execution in 1989. And, even today, seeing Bundy's face in the media sparks chilling flashbacks of the tan-clothed man who politely asked her, 'Can you point me in the right direction?'

But while Tricia will never forget her terrifying encounter with Bundy, it also fuelled her fascination for true crime – an 'obsession' that would ultimately lead to her owning the crime blogger site Websleuths.com, three decades later. Tightly moderated with a strict 'No rumours' policy, the forum today has 200,000 members who converge online to discuss and investigate unsolved crimes and missing person cases. The international network comprises an impressive smorgasbord of experts. As Tricia explains: 'We don't look for members, they come to us. We have nurses, doctors, surgeons, retired law enforcement officers. An ink specialist joined us. And we have psychologists, psychiatrists, a person that owns a company that tries to pinpoint crimes using satellite pictures. We have people from all walks of life. They're amazing. I love them all.'

Tricia has an infectious, down-to-earth personality. When we meet online a second time, she's peering into a light-up vanity mirror, colouring her mouth with a wand of peachy lip balm. 'Can you just give me a second, dear,' she says, 'I just gotta put a bit of this on.' She puts down the balm and uses her thumbs to wipe beneath her eyes. 'Oh, Lord. Come on, Tricia, you can do better than that.' I disagree; Tricia is a vibrant vision alongside my February-in-London pallor in the online meeting room gallery. I could pass for the ghoulish figure in Edvard Munch's *The Scream*, whereas Tricia's rocking the pre-Raphaelite look, with frothy blonde locks pouring over her shoulders beneath the grip of an Alice band festooned with silk flowers. She looks into the camera. 'OK, we are good to go.'

Alongside the discussion forum, Tricia also hosts the Websleuths YouTube Livestream shows in her pine-walled sitting room in Dallas, Texas. This is where she's joining me from today. Snuggled on the sofa beside the Websleuths owner is her beloved dog, Scrappy Joe, a chiweenie (a dachshund-chihuahua cross breed), and her two cats, Lilith and Boo. 'Scrappy Joe's a little internet star – he sits with me during my livestreams. Scrappy Joe and the cats are all cutie pies. They're always with me when I'm working, jumping on me – they're very much a part of it.'

A collection of quirky knick-knacks huddle on the shelf behind the sofa, including a Ruth Bader Ginsberg puppet, and a Bernie Sanders doll imprisoned in an empty mayonnaise jar. 'That's just me being silly,' says Tricia. 'But really, this room is the heartbeat of Websleuths – and we take our work very seriously.'

Tricia's journey into online sleuthing was a circuitous affair, incorporating a twenty-year career as a radio DJ, marriage, motherhood and the ensuing tedium of 'being stuck in the house all day.'

'After recognising Ted Bundy in the *Salt Lake Tribune* article, I became obsessed with true crime. Throughout the eighties, I pored over news stories and read any true crime book I could lay my hands on. One book that piqued my interest most was Ann Rule's *The Stranger Beside Me* which, of course, charted Rule's personal relationship with Ted Bundy. I devoured that book – I practically memorised it.

'In the early nineties, I became hooked on the channel, *Lifetime: Television for Women*. I remember there was a show about women who'd killed their husbands – it was great. Then, in 1996, two key life events happened: the radio station where I worked changed its format and fired everybody – myself included – and, after seventeen years of marriage, my husband and I decided to try for a baby. Well, I got pregnant immediately.

'Our son Will was born in September 1996 and, although being an extremely proud mom, by early December of that year I felt I was losing my mind. I was home morning, noon and night – and newborn babies, well, they eat, sleep, cry, pee, poo, laugh and cry some more. I had little contact with the outside world – I was literally climbing the walls.'

One day at the end of December 1996, after settling her son for a mid-morning nap, Tricia sat down to read a local newspaper. A headline grabbed her attention: 'Six-year-old beauty queen found dead in her basement.'

'I thought, this had to be a mistake,' says Tricia. 'There are no *six*-year-old beauty queens. It must be a typo. Surely, it was meant to read "*Sixteen*-year-old beauty queen found dead in her basement".'

The newspaper article was 'teeny', according to Tricia. A few paragraphs at most: the girl's name was JonBenét Ramsey, whose body was discovered by a family member at their home in Boulder, Colorado, on the afternoon of 26 December 1996. JonBenét had not been shot or stabbed but Boulder Police Chief Tom Koby considered her death 'a homicide'.

Intrigued, Tricia turned to her new encyclopaedia, the novel technological source from which she could discover information the television news channels often omitted: the internet. She switched on her clunky computer and waited impatiently, assailed by the cranky bleeps and gargles of the dial-up modem. Once connected to the web, Tricia grabbed her mouse, clicked on the Internet Explorer icon, then typed the words: 'JonBenét Ramsey, beauty queen, murdered, Colorado' into the search box. Tricia scrolled through the results. Already, the web was awash with news of JonBenét's death – and a photograph of the victim validated the newspaper report. It was JonBenét – a little girl made up to look twenty-something in scarlet lipstick and blue eyeshadow, a beauty queen sash crossing her little chest. 'I couldn't believe it. This pretty little girl was in full make-up.' Tricia trawled, clicked and absorbed with sadness and frustration the mysterious chain of events surrounding the tragic death of the little girl at her family home whilst it was festooned with Christmas decorations.

JonBenét was last seen alive by her parents John and Patsy Ramsey when she went to bed on Christmas evening, reports said. The following morning, Patsy got up to make coffee around 5.30 a.m. and allegedly found a two-and-a-half-page ransom note on a back staircase of the house. The letter said JonBenét had been kidnapped, demanded $118,000 in cash and warned: 'Do not contact police.' Patsy called 911 and reported her daughter missing. Investigators then launched a kidnapping probe. Eight hours later, Boulder detective Linda Arndt asked John Ramsey and family friend Fleet White to search the house for 'anything amiss.' John then found his daughter's body in a basement spare room where he and Patsy had hidden Christmas presents. JonBenét had been gagged with duct tape and strangled with a garrotte.

As days and weeks passed, Tricia engrossed herself in the JonBenét case. She watched every television news report and scoured the internet for updates while bouncing Will on her knee. Tricia's online research led her to a JonBenét discussion forum. Eagerly scanning the posts, she realised she'd found a community of people like her – baffled yet inquisitive, with one common question: 'Who killed JonBenét Ramsey?'

Initially, Tricia felt intimidated by the forum members' discussions. They were articulate and intelligent, and their posts conveyed an air of authority. 'Oh my God, those people were so smart. I knew nothing about this stuff back then, but I was totally obsessed with this forum.' Eventually, Tricia mustered the courage to type her first post – a question: 'When did John Ramsey turn on the light and see JonBenét's body?' Those twelve words heralded the start of Tricia's illustrious sleuthing career. 'That was it, I was hooked,' she says.

Two years later, Tricia established her own crime discussion forum called ForumsForJustice.org, which is still active. Focussing on the JonBenét case, the forum aims to discredit scandalous accusations made against innocent suspects while highlighting those who were never thoroughly investigated. This discussion surrounding the mystery of JonBenét's death would continue with prominence on Websleuths when Tricia bought the site for $1500 in 2004. It's a case that still consumes Websleuthers today. When I ask Tricia, 'Who do you think killed JonBenét?' she momentarily closes her eyes and nods slowly.

'I am absolutely going to go on the record with this. First, what I *can* say, is that there was no intruder. I believe that Patsy wrote the ransom note. And I believe what happened to JonBenét was an accident. There was no intention to murder her.'

'Websleuths has done some great stuff on the JonBenét case,' she tells me. Tricia goes on to cite the work of Cina Wong, a forensic handwriting expert and Websleuth member who examined the JonBenét ransom note in 2016. Cina spent three weeks comparing the calligraphy in the letter to the hundred handwriting samples Patsy Ramsey submitted to police. 'We reached out to Cina to investigate the samples,' adds Tricia. 'The work she's done is amazing. Cina found over two hundred and eighty examples of the ransom note matching her [Patsy's] writing. The ransom writer made their "qs" exactly like the number eight, it was a weird thing. Patsy Ramsey, in her regular handwriting, also made a small "q" like the letter eight. I mean, you look at that and go, wow, that's just too wild.'

Cina concluded it was 'highly probable' that the ransom note was written by Patsy Ramsey. She found that the ransom note and Patsy's samples contained four variations of the letter 'a'. In both pieces of writing Cina also noted how the letters 't' and 'e' 'connected and touched' where they appeared together on the page.

'Meanwhile,' Tricia continues, 'when evidence emerged regarding the varying sizes of JonBenét's underwear, other Websleuthers conducted experiments on underwear sizes. They also put together incredible timelines that were just so detailed and perfect.'

Tricia is rightly proud of the site's 'No dramas' reputation amongst members – unlike some other online sleuthers, she says, who 'turn up at victims' houses and scream at them with foghorn.' And she is quick to humbly point out that Websleuths is not a 'crime-solving' unit.

'It's the law enforcement agencies' job to solve crimes,' she says. 'At Websleuths, members use their expertise to gather evidence that might be helpful to investigations or cold cases. We only work with information available in the public domain – information released by police and news outlets. We wouldn't want to harm an investigation – that's the last thing we want.

'But there's some shocking sleuthing going on out there. There's this one guy – I won't name him – a retired cop who's putting out all this false information and doing horrible things. It's the same with Facebook; most of the true crime pages on Facebook are just all drama. Then the police think we [Websleuthers] are just like them, and we are not.

'We now have ten administrators at Websleuths who thoroughly verify all new members and moderate the group's postings. Our rules are simple: no rumours; no naming (unless police have confirmed somebody as a suspect) or shaming; and stick to the facts.'

Websleuths' credible reputation was not built overnight. In its early days, the group was rife with bullies spouting inaccurate theories. 'When I purchased the site in 2004 it was a snake pit. There were about two hundred and fifty members and they were all threatening one another: "You suck"; "You're horrible"; "I know where you live" – that kind of thing. There was so much drama, it made me sick.

'So, in 2008, we tightened the rules. We banned all the troublemakers – because I knew that if we got enough *good* people, we really could make a difference. But some members didn't like this. They left the group. and, honest to God, I really thought Websleuths would fail. I thought, *"I'm an idiot."* Well, what happened is people came out of the woodwork and joined the group. They were thankful. Then, in July 2008, a little girl called Caylee Anthony disappeared – and Websleuths exploded.'

The story gripped America. On 15 July, two-year-old Caylee Anthony was reported missing from her home in Orlando, Florida. The toddler's grandmother, Cindy Anthony, made the frantic emergency call. She had just confronted her daughter and Caylee's mother, Casey Anthony, who at first claimed her little girl was with a babysitter. Casey, a twenty-two-year-old single mother, then changed her story and admitted her daughter had vanished thirty-one days earlier.

Two days before Cindy called police, she and her husband George received a letter saying that Casey's abandoned car had been impounded in a tow yard. George collected the vehicle, which contained Caylee's car seat and toys, and Casey's purse. But what struck him most was the sickening aroma emanating from the boot. It smelled of decomposing organic matter, he thought – a stench so overpowering that he had to drive the car home with its windows wound down. During her 911 call, Cindy told the operator: 'Caylee's missing. I found my daughter's car today. It smells like there's been a dead body in there.'

The following day, Casey Anthony was arrested on charges of child neglect. When questioned by detectives at Orange County Jail, she told a string of lies. Casey claimed she worked as an event planner at Universal Studios. She then embellished her babysitter story, claiming that Caylee had been kidnapped by her 'nanny', Zenaida 'Zanny' Gonzalez. Casey said she'd tried to find her daughter but had been 'too frazzled' to report her disappearance to the police. Detectives soon established that Casey had fabricated her 'job' at Universal – and she didn't have a nanny for Caylee.

Casey was jailed for giving false statements to law enforcement, child neglect and obstructing a criminal investigation. She was released in August 2008 after a Californian bounty hunter footed her $500,000 bail bond.

A month later, as the hunt for Caylee continued, FBI investigators found traces of chloroform in the boot of Casey's car. Air sample tests from the trunk also revealed evidence of human decomposition. In October, a grand jury charged Casey with first-degree murder, aggravated child abuse, aggravated manslaughter of a child, and four counts of providing false information to police.

Meanwhile, thousands of volunteers had joined the police search for Caylee, whose remains were eventually found, stuffed in a rubbish bag, in woods close to the Anthony family home in December 2008.

At Casey's sensational 2011 murder trial, jurors heard how the mum had partied and entered a 'hot body' contest at a local club four days after Caylee vanished. Seeking the death penalty, the prosecution alleged that Casey killed her daughter by drugging her with chloroform and covering her nose and mouth with duct tape. Casey searched the internet eighty-four times for 'chloroform', as well as 'neck breaking' and 'household weapons', the prosecution further claimed.

Casey's defence argued that Caylee accidentally drowned in the family's swimming pool on 16 June, 2008. The jury accepted this theory and acquitted Casey of first-degree murder. She wept in the dock as the Orange County Courthouse clerk read out guilty verdicts for misdemeanour counts of providing false information to a law enforcement officer. Casey was released from jail on 17 July, 2011.

'Caylee Anthony's death was certainly one of the biggest cases on Websleuths,' Tricia recalls. 'Florida's Sunshine Law means police must release every piece of evidence from a case – unless there's an order not to. Websleuths blasted into the stratosphere with this – and I'm referring to our members, not me. They did amazing work. Based on Casey Anthony's phone records, they created a "ping" map. Now, it's done easily, but back then it hadn't been done. The map showed exactly where Casey Anthony was, compared to where she *said* she was. The difference wasn't even close.

'Our members also asked for the searches officers found on Casey Anthony's computer. The sleuths studied those documents in detail – and found further searches made by Anthony via other search engines. One result showed a search for "foolproof suffocation" shortly before Caylee disappeared. I think this information could have made a huge difference to the prosecution's case.'

Orange County Captain Angelo Nieves later admitted that his investigators had missed the Google search for 'foolproof suffocation' methods made in the Anthony home on the day Caylee was last seen alive. 'One of the detectives who worked on the Anthony case actually came on to the forum and posted a message, thanking members for their efforts, adds Tricia. 'He was really sweet.' Tricia knows the forum's threads are followed by detectives from all corners of the world. 'They won't always admit they're following us – but I know they are. I see their IP addresses.'

Websleuths has achieved some major successes, and one such breakthrough happened in 2009 as the group discussed the vanishing of forty-two-year-old Abraham Shakespeare, who'd won thirty-million dollars in the Florida lottery three years previously. The casual labourer had been down to his last three dollars before he scooped the jackpot. Abraham's relatives hoped he'd jetted off to the Caribbean with his winnings when they reported him missing in November 2009, although nobody had seen him since April.

As the forum's debate on Abraham's disappearance gathered momentum, Sleuthers became suspicious of a prevalent poster in the thread – a woman named Dorice 'Dee Dee' Moore, who'd befriended Abraham. Moore had come into Abraham's life in 2008, claiming to be an author working on a book about his rags-to-riches story and how people had 'taken advantage' of him. Now, Abraham was missing – and Moore had taken over the lottery winner's assets, including his million dollar mansion in Lakeland, Florida.

Before his disappearance, officially, Moore had become Abraham's financial advisor, but according to her posts on Websleuths, the pair were also 'best friends'. Sick of constant attention from 'gold diggers', Abraham had gone to ground, Moore claimed.

Tricia was instantly wary of Moore, who initially posted under her real name. 'Moore was this flashy woman who said she was a close friend of Abraham. She said she'd helped Abraham get out of town and that he'd granted her power of attorney of his affairs. "I'm taking care of his money," she declared. Then, as evidence mounted against Moore – one member managed to obtain her bank records – I received a private email from her [Moore]. She promptly denied it was her posting on Websleuths, claiming somebody else was fraudulently using her name. I knew she was lying, so I replied to Moore's email. I wrote, "Well, I gotta tell you, somebody must have broken into your house and used your computer – because the IP address on this email matches the IP address of the Dee Dee Moore postings."'

Armed with this damning information, Tricia made a rare exception to her 'no naming or shaming' policy and posted one sentence on Websleuths' Abraham Shakespeare thread: 'Dee Dee Moore killed him [Abraham].'

'Wow, Moore got mad at that. She started posting again, contesting every piece of incriminating evidence stacked against her. Moore went on to claim that her computer had been hacked. Her actions simply galvanised our suspicions. Moore was a scam artist – and I was convinced she killed Abraham Shakespeare.'

Tricia's instincts were spot-on. In January 2010, Moore became a 'person of interest' when detectives found Abraham's body in her boyfriend's backyard. Abraham had been shot twice in the chest – then buried in a five-foot deep dirt trench beneath a newly-constructed patio. Moore was convicted of first-degree murder and sentenced to life in prison without parole.

Around the time of Moore's arrest, a detective who worked on the murder probe wrote to Tricia and thanked the Websleuths members for their hard work. But Florida Police later insisted no officer had logged on to Websleuths, Tricia is convinced that law enforcement officers *had* followed the Abraham Shakespeare discussion. 'It was infuriating,' recalls Tricia, her face darkening as Scrappy Joe jumps onto her lap and turns towards the camera, his little brow knotted with worry. 'The detective on the case actually emailed me and told me what a great job we'd done. And then a few years later, when *Rolling Stone* magazine wanted to write an article about Websleuths' involvement, the police department released a statement saying we did nothing on the Abraham Shakespeare case – which was a total lie. For some reason somebody got hold of that detective who contacted me – and he got his behind chewed. It's frustrating when law enforcement agencies don't take us seriously.'

One of Tricia's main goals, she says, is to 'drag law enforcement, kicking and screaming, into the twenty-first century.' 'We're not "beer can-collecting housewives",' – which was how John Ramsey described Websleuthers years ago – 'But that's the problem: most law enforcement agencies think we're just a bunch of interfering biddies, so they don't want anything to do with us.

'Oh, my God, some days I just want to pull the sheet up over my head and not even get up. It is so frustrating; we're not trying to take anybody's jobs away. But when you have a whole army of people from all over the world, with different life experiences, they can look at things differently and they can help – and they want to do this for free.

'I'm just perplexed as to why police won't come to us more often and let us help them. You know, give us that crappy piece of evidence from an unsolved case that no one wants to deal with anymore. Our members will love it. They will tear it apart and find what you need. And I have the perfect example to prove this fact.'

Tricia tells me that she was pleasantly surprised when a detective in Nevada contacted the forum for help on a murder case that had gone cold – as she stresses, it's rare for law enforcement to employ the hive mind of Websleuths. The victim, a male hiker, had been found with stab wounds in the mountains of Nevada in 1992. For twenty-three years police had tried to gather evidence about a T-shirt the victim had on, significant for its eagle emblem.

Tricia posted a picture of the T-shirt on the forum and Websleuthers spent ten fruitless days investigating – until a member who had been away returned to the forum and cracked the riddle within thirty-six hours. 'Oh, that was a proud moment,' says Tricia, smiling. 'The woman who solved this had just returned from vacation. She found out the manufacturer, where the T-shirt was sold – it was still on sale up to 2014 – and who shipped it to the store. She even found out its original price. Imagine. The police had been trying to solve this for twenty-three years – then one of our members got hold of this piece of evidence and provided all the information they needed within thirty-six hours. This information didn't lead to the identity of the victim but at least police could check this evidence off their list and move on.'

The community spirit and enthusiasm among Websleuthers leaps off the forum's website page. Members are quick to congratulate their peers' successes as they work together on thousands of threads. It's this community spirit – and the impact the team has on cases – that drives members, says Tricia. 'People see Websleuths as a community where their voices can be heard. All they want to do is just help. They want to feel like they are contributing – and they can do this right there at home on their computers.'

At the end of our interview, Tricia stresses that she'd like to thank those members. She lifts Scrappy Joe off her lap and clasps her hands in front of her throat in a gesture of complete sincerity. 'Without our moderators and members, Websleuths would be nothing. They do all of the work and I love every one of them. They're my true crime angels.'

5

The Mother Lode

Paul Haynes, a respectable, law-abiding, articulate citizen of Los Angeles, had never pictured himself pulling off a heist. Even now – driving south on the Santa Ana Freeway in a gleaming black SUV, his partner on this mission behind him driving a matching vehicle – he questioned whether they'd make their getaway from Orange County Sheriff Department's headquarters with their valuable haul. '*Hmm, that's if we* get *our haul.*'

'Exit ahead at junction 105 B,' said the satnav, 'Then, turn right onto North Broadway.' Nerves and excitement brewed in Paul's stomach.

His vehicle glided between pavements sprouting palm trees, as he forked into West Civic Center Drive, then took a left onto N. Flower Street and swished into the car park at number 550 – the Orange County Sheriff's Department. 'You have reached your destination.'

Paul switched off the engine, flipped down the sun visor then thumbed a text message to his accomplice, Michele McNamara. 'Just arrived. You here yet?'

Speech bubbles hiccupped on the screen. 'Just parking up.' When he looked up, Michelle was there, waving through the window of the SUV parked beside him in the loading bay behind the Orange County Sheriff's Department building. They locked their cars and walked to the entrance.

'You ready?' said Michelle, nudging Paul's side, a look of exhilaration on her face.

'Yeah, absolutely,' said Paul. *'I'm actually going on a heist. This is huge. This is* Ocean's Eleven,' he thought to himself.

Well, what they were there to do wasn't *technically* a heist. Paul and Michelle were not armed. They did not plan to pull stockings over their heads and charge into the sheriff's office shouting, 'Show us the safe!' That said, a lot rested on them accomplishing their goal: to sneak into the records room marked 'EARONS' and seize the 'Mother Lode' — thirty-seven containers holding forty years of evidence relating to the crimes of an unidentified prolific rapist and serial killer — before piling their consignment into the SUVs and making off. All without being caught by sheriff officials. Just another day at the office for the two citizen investigators.

It was January 2016 and Paul had spent the last five years obsessively researching reams of data with Michelle in their pursuit to unmask the killer-rapist who had terrorised America's Golden State in the seventies and eighties. During those decades, the media coined several nicknames for the criminal, the two most prevalent being the East Area Rapist and the Original Night Stalker. The two titles were then abbreviated and combined to form EARONS.

Michelle had cleared the secret mission to obtain the EARONS files with one of her many detective sources, she'd assured Paul. But as the pair entered the law enforcement headquarters, sceptical thoughts clouded his excitement. *'Wait a minute, law enforcement agencies don't let private citizens take what they want, do they?'*

Detectives had spent years trying to identify a suspect in the EARONS case – a man who who'd raped dozens of women and murdered at least thirteen people across eleven counties in California. After his last known slaying in 1986, the killer vanished. Now, the police investigation had stagnated. The EARONS records room had lain untouched for years – a tomb remembering bloodshed and heartache without any justice served. Paul and Michelle believed they could advance or possibly solve the case – if their plan to extract this evidence was successful.

Today, Paul maintains a composed posture as he remembers that day. 'When Michelle suggested we motorcade into Santa Ana in two SUVs with the expectation that we would be leaving with the Mother Lode – as we'd dubbed the EARONS evidence – I was dubious but more than willing to give it a shot,' he says via video link from his home in Los Angeles, where he's lived since 2015. The South-Floridian writer and data miner settles back on his sofa beneath a framed *Wings of Desire* movie poster. He has dusty blond hair, serious eyes and a mind like a database. 'I followed Michelle into the Orange County Sheriff's Department building, still feeling dubious, but also excited at the prospect that we might just pull this off. Michelle's contact ushered us into an office. We chatted for about forty minutes – well, I let Michelle do the talking. I can't disclose the source's name or reveal what was said in that office, but I will say this: in the space of forty minutes, I felt the energy in the room shift from smug scepticism to awe. Then Michelle's source led us to the EARONS property room.'

Detectives, both retired and serving, trusted true crime writer Michelle and valued her input on the case that had consumed her since 2010. Michelle had long maintained public interest in the languishing EARONS investigation, which she first wrote about in her *True Crime Diary* blog. 'The great tragedy for me with this case is that it's not better known,' she wrote in 2011. The case deserved more 'heat' she stated. Michelle had worked round-the-clock on her 'murder habit' from her desk in her daughter's playroom, which she'd converted into a research unit. Michelle was willing to go to extreme lengths in her bid to solve the EARONS mystery – as was evidenced on this day when she and Paul stepped into the windowless closet housing a 'treasure trove' of evidence.

The overhead fluorescent strip bulb woke from its coma, flickering its light upon shelves stacked with bankers boxes now furred with dust. Surrounded by the Mother Lode, Paul and Michelle fell silent for a few seconds, both thinking, *'How are we going to shift this lot?'* The room heaved with labelled containers containing the remnants of shattered and snuffed-out lives. There were sixty-five boxes in total – plus two oversized bins – all rammed with documents.

While the unnamed detective kept guard, the two investigators foraged in the boxes, identifying information they were going to 'borrow' that might shine light on their probe. Paul explains, 'Much of this information had not been seen by active police investigators on the case, so we were keen to delve into the overlooked copies of reports in the hope that somewhere, in the margins, we'd find a clue that would lead us to a name for the EARONS suspect.'

But there was no time to thoroughly scrutinise the material at that point; should a department official happen upon the rummaging strangers in the closet, they would certainly leave empty-handed – and be hauled over the coals by the powers that be.

Paul's expression remains cool when he tells me what happened next. Although I do detect a quiver of nostalgic excitement at the corners of his mouth. 'We decided to borrow thirty-five bankers boxes and the two bins, but we had to act fast. We loaded the containers onto dollies, wheeled them out to the loading bay then piled the boxes into the back of the

SUVs. We did this several times, running back and forth with the dollies. At one point, when we were loading the cars, the undersheriff appeared. He came out of the building. Now our mission definitely felt like a heist. Michelle was like, "Y'know, let's pick up the pace and get out of here before people change their minds." Fortunately, the undersheriff was far enough away and was unaware of what was unfolding in the loading bay. But I was fully aware of the magnitude of what Michelle and I were being entrusted with. I felt anxious. We stacked the last of the boxes into the cars – then drove away, seemingly undetected.'

The pair decided to store the files at Michelle's house in Los Feliz, Los Angeles, where she lived with her actor-comedian husband, Patton Oswalt, and their seven-year-old daughter, Alice. 'The playroom became the Box Room,' says Paul. 'And I would borrow several boxes at a time to share the workload. Michelle believed there to be around an 80 per cent chance that the offender's name would appear in the documents contained in those boxes. Obtaining those files was the most exciting break in the investigation. A game-changer.' Michelle bought two high-volume digital scanners and the independent investigators got stuck into the mountainous job of examining the Mother Lode.

At that time, the FBI agreed with Michelle's theory that the EARONS killer was responsible for three crime sprees throughout California, with the first in this series beginning in April 1974 in Visalia, an agricultural city nestled in the San Joaquin Valley.

A serial burglar known only as the Visalia Ransacker perplexed police with his bizarre modus operandi. The Visalia Ransacker was no ordinary burglar. He prowled the city's dark streets and alleys, targeting ranch houses and bungalows whose doors and windows were left unlocked by trusting residents. Unlike most thieves who act swiftly, this intruder appeared to be in no hurry. Sometimes, he'd stay inside properties for hours, raiding wardrobes and drawers and vandalising possessions. He scattered women's underwear and pilfered personal items such as photographs, wedding rings, coins and kids' piggy banks. A single earring was taken on one occasion. But strangely, he chose not to steal more expensive belongings, or even take banknotes. The Visalia Ransacker is believed to have broken into more than a hundred homes across four communities in the city.

During one episode in September 1975, he went armed with a .38 calibre handgun he'd stolen from another property. The burglar crept into the bedroom of Elizabeth Hupp at 2 a.m., pointed the pistol at her and woke the terrified sixteen-year-old. 'You're coming with me,' he growled through the mouth hole of his ski mask. 'Don't make a noise or I'll kill you.'

As the prowler hustled Elizabeth out the back door, the noise woke her father, Claude Snelling, a College of the Sequoias journalism professor. Snelling leapt from his bed and hurried outside to find the masked man dragging his daughter across the patio. 'What are you doing? Where are you taking my daughter?' he yelled. The kidnapper threw Elizabeth to the ground then fired his gun twice at Claude. He then kicked the teenage girl three times in the face before vaulting a fence and sprinting off. The attacker fled and Claude died on his way to hospital.

Detective Bill McGowen was one of the officers assigned to the Visalia Ransacker case. As his son, Brett, would later attest, Bill dedicated his life to the investigation – and one night he almost caught the serial burglar. In the early hours of 10 December, 1975, Bill was on a stakeout on West Kaweah Avenue, Visalia, following a tip-off from neighbours. Hiding in a resident's garage, Bill spotted a masked man peering through a window of house previously targeted by the mystery plunderer. Bill drew his gun and torch and powered from his hiding place. 'Stop,' he shouted, throwing a spear of flashlight into the stalker's eyes.

The suspect peeled off his ski mask and begged, 'Please. Don't hurt me.' He sounded like a frightened child, his voice high and squeaky. He raised one hand as though to surrender, then plunged his free hand into his pocket, pulled out a gun and fired it at Bill's flashlight. The torch exploded as the bullet hit it, blowing him backwards in a shower of broken glass. Shards flew into his eyes as he hit the ground. He could no longer see the gunman, but he heard the hurried whumps of his feet, and the sound of wood straining as he jumped over a fence.

Later that day, Bill spoke to *Action News* about the shooting. His right eye patched, the seasoned detective looked visibly shaken as he relived the moment he came face to face with the ransacker. He said: 'I fell down. The impact [of the torch exploding] knocked me back and he continued to run, throwing some items apparently taken in the area.'

After the second shooting, the bizarre burglaries in Visalia suddenly stopped, leaving behind a city scarred and violated by the crimes. Then, a new wave of unbelievable sickening violence engulfed the northern Californian capital. In mid 1976, the residents of Sacramento County quaked with terror as a serial rapist haunted eastern subdivisions surrounding Mather Air Force Base. Gun and lock sales in the area went through the roof as the community were terrified by the spectre of the man the police and media dubbed the East Area Rapist. People bought guard dogs. Many slept with shotguns beneath their pillows.

The predator stalked his victims and staked out occupied, one-storey ranch houses. He severed phone lines and climbed through windows, often in the dead of night and would wake his victims with the blinding glare of his flashlight. He initially targeted women he knew to be home alone. Survivors reported that the fiend always wore a ski mask and gloves and spoke 'through clenched teeth'. 'Shut up or I'll kill you,' he'd growl as he straddled women on their beds. His victims couldn't see his face, but they could hear his dense breaths and they could smell his musty odour. Armed with a sharpened butcher knife and a gun, the East Area Rapist blindfolded and bound his female victims with shoelaces or twine before sexually assaulting them.

By 1977, he had progressed to attacking families or couples in several regions of Northern California. After breaking into a couple's home, he would silence the husband with a gun before tying him up and stacking plates on his back. Then he'd rape the bound man's wife in another room while repeating evil threats to kill them both if he heard the crockery rattle or smash. Some women were sodomised in those horrific and sustained assaults.

The East Area Rapist also ransacked his victims' homes and then lurked for hours, often helping himself to food and beer before raping the women again. He would steal precious belongings – jewellery, family photographs, ID cards, house keys and ornaments – trophies to remind him of his heinous acts. Sometimes, the beast would burst into tears and sob after molesting a woman or girl. But if this was remorse then it was short-lived as he would callously move on to his next helpless rape victim.

In 1977, as detectives ramped up their efforts to catch the rapist, he taunted them with threats he made via telephone calls to police stations. 'I'm the East Area Rapist. I have my next victim already stalked and you guys can't catch me,' he said. The rapist would also make chilling calls to the women he'd attacked. 'I'm gonna kill you,' he'd rasp. A year later, the rapist killed for the first time.

Around 9 p.m. on 2 February, 1978, newlyweds Brian Maggiore and his wife, Katie, were accosted by a man in a ski mask while walking their dog in Sacramento's Rancho Cordova area. After a confrontation, the couple fled, but the stranger gave chase and then shot them dead. At the time, investigators suspected it was the East Area Rapist who had killed the Maggiores. Not only had the slayings happened in his preferred territory, but a shoelace had been found at the scene of the double murder. The shoelace was tied in a double loop that could be used like handcuffs – just like the restraints used by the East Area Rapist.

The rapes briefly ceased following the Rancho Cordova killings but resumed in 1979 with attacks on women, young girls and couples in Santa Barbara, over 300 miles south of Sacramento. The EAR, as he became known for short, committed twenty more rapes before again progressing to murder.

On 30 December, 1979, osteopathic surgeon Robert Offerman and his girlfriend Alexandria Manning, a clinical psychologist, were bound and shot in Robert's home in Goleta, near Santa Barbara. As the eighties dawned, the EAR's killing career began to escalate, earning him his new sobriquet of Night Stalker. He was later renamed the Original Night Stalker (ONS for short) to differentiate him from another serial killer, Richard Ramirez.

The Original Night Stalker had the same twisted penchant for raping women in front of their husbands or partners but now he would not leave his victims alive. After raping the women victims, he would kill both them and their partners. He went on to strike again in Santa Barbara, Ventura and Orange Counties. There were seven more murder victims between March 1980 and July 1981. The executioner used a fireplace log to bludgeon Lyman Smith and his wife Charlene in their Ventura County home. In Dana Point, Patrice and Keith Harrington were also beaten dead with a blunt object. Manuela Witthun was raped and beaten to death in her home in Irvine. Cheri Domingo and Gregory Sanchez were murdered in bed in Goleta in 1981. Then the murders suddenly stopped – until the ONS killed for the last known time. In May 1986, a real estate agent found the naked body of eighteen-year-old Janelle Cruz in her blood-soaked bed. She had been home alone when the ONS broke in. After raping Janelle, he beat her to death. Police believed the ONS bludgeoned her with a pipe wrench.

Initially, detectives hunting the EAR and ONS respectively didn't link the two crime sprees to one individual. It wasn't until 2001 that DNA testing established that the EAR and ONS sprees had been committed by one man. This revelation inspired the creation of California's DNA database, which collects genetic samples from all accused and convicted felons in the state.

* * *

Most of the amateur investigators I met while writing this book said their interest in sleuthing stemmed from an earlier event or experience – be it a terrifying encounter with a serial killer, the murder of a loved one or a brutal killing in their neighbourhood. For some, it is simply a cold case they've read about that they can't let go. For Paul Haynes, a 'cloistered and dysfunctional' upbringing in Plantation, South Florida, complete with a stark warning from his father about a serial killer, triggered his investigative drive.

Paul was eighteen when John Edward Robinson was arrested and charged in 2000 for the murders of women he'd lured online for sadomasochistic sex. The decaying bodies of three women were found stuffed in oil drums on Robinson's farm in Kansas. A further two corpses were recovered from a nearby storage locker. Often referred to as the 'first internet killer', Robinson was later sentenced to the death penalty.

'I had long been interested in mysteries and unsolved crimes,' says Paul, 'but I don't think this was fully realised until my father alerted me to the Robinson murders, which were all over the news at the time. I had a troubled home life, so I wasn't socially well adjusted. Because my friends were mainly people I met online, my father told me to be cautious of those I was connecting with in cyber space.

'Robinson lured his victims to his property – and then they disappeared. To me, this was an intriguing news story. Robinson had presented himself as a pillar of the community: a churchgoer and successful businessman. In reality, he was a depraved serial murderer. That contrast between his public persona and who he really was, fascinated me. I began reading about other serial killer cases, especially unsolved ones. I tried to imagine who the perpetrators might be. This interest would wax and wane over the years but it never really left me.'

Paul first learned about the mystery surrounding the EAR's barbarities via a television special in 2006. Back then, Paul was studying film and media at Florida Atlantic University and had no intentions of becoming an 'armchair sleuth' (he air-quotes this designation for effect). The documentary focussed on the rape attacks in northern California – crimes previously unknown to Paul. He went online to investigate further, and the information that emerged stunned him.

'I was staggered to discover that the suspect was linked to around fifty rapes and at least twelve murders. But I was also stunned at how a case of this scope had not reached a wider level of public interest. I set up a Google news alert for EARONS – as I had done so for many other unsolved cases – so I could keep up with what was happening.'

But the EARONS cases puzzled Paul. How could this suspect – one of the biggest serial offenders in modern history – still be at large? Who was he? And what had driven him to commit these horrendous crimes? As years passed with seemingly little new light cast on the rape and murder series, Paul began his own research into the case that had stymied law enforcement ranks for over three decades.

'After film school I moved to New York for a year, but things didn't work out, so I moved back to Florida and got a job at a legal firm. There was a lot of downtime in that role, so I used it to begin some research into the EARONS crimes. A year later, the legal firm closed, so, at twenty-eight, I found myself back in South Florida, living with my parents. And that's when I started looking more deeply into the case.'

Paul's interest in EARONS soon morphed into an obsession that saw him spending up to fifteen hours a day online.

'What interested me about EARONS was the geographic sequence of the offences. The suspect operated in a two-to-three-year window of time in a specific area of northern California. And then he offended in another place in northern California, plus [there was] a five-to-six-year period offending in different communities in southern California. So, it got me thinking about public records and online resources – information that wasn't available to the public in the days when the offences were committed. He was an active offender, but the EARONS series were not connected until 2001. So, this suspect had quite a head start.

'I began by looking for people who lived in the same geographical areas during the periods when the offender was active. I searched classmates.com, Intelius [a public records business], Ancestry.com and other public records and aggregators. I also searched for people who might not have been on law enforcement's radar at the time because maybe they didn't have a criminal history or lived in a different area to where the crimes took place.

'I started putting more time into my research. I was in a state of depression back then, so I became absorbed with this case. For instance, I would scan yearbooks from Sacramento, year by year: 1968, 1972, 1973, etc. I looked at senior white males – because I knew the offender was a white male – and I plugged their names into public records to determine where they lived. I used court records to see whether those individuals had any criminal connection that made them more interesting. I looked to see whether the names were connected to the military, law enforcement or medical industries. Speculation at the time hinted that the EARONS may have worked in these fields.

'I told myself I wouldn't put excess time or money into this research, but I found myself doing so anyway. And the more I did it, the more I realised I was good at finding people. Instead of marinating in my depression, I kind of drifted into doing this full-time – and I found there were people worth considering as potential suspects in this series.'

Paul's research centred on data mining. He digitised telephone directories, compiled master lists from birth, death and marriage records, and studied reverse directories. Initially Paul felt embarrassed about his investigative work, which threw up several 'red herrings' and led him down internet 'rabbit holes'. He posted his theories on message forums, although he was mindful not to 'cry wolf', even when he did stumble across a potential suspect. He says, 'I didn't communicate with police because I hadn't come across a strong enough suspect – and at that point I thought citizen detectives were generally regarded with a degree of contempt by law enforcement agencies. If I were to reach out, it would need to be with a name I strongly believed could be a suspect.'

At the time, he was an avid follower of Michelle's *True Crime Diary* blog. Paul posted a link to her 2011 EARONS entry titled *Who Are You?* in a discussion forum maintained by A&E, a television network that specialises in true crime documentaries. Michelle, a regular contributor to the A&E group, replied to Paul's post. She'd followed his previous messages and was hugely impressed by his tenacity, observing how the keen investigator had spent nearly four thousand hours data mining for a possible breakthrough. The pair started swapping information and they fast became a unique team. Michelle, then forty-one, nicknamed Paul, then twenty-nine, 'The Kid'. She would later write: 'The Kid is smart, meticulous and the case's greatest amateur hope.'

Paul felt an instant affinity with his co-investigator. He even spent Thanksgiving 2012 with Michelle, helping her to craft a longform article about EARONS for *Los Angeles Magazine*. 'In the Footsteps of a Killer' was published in February 2013 to much critical acclaim. In the piece, Michelle lay bare the perverted sins of the EARONS attacker – and gave him a new moniker. From that moment, the man who'd wreaked tragic carnage up and down California would be known as the Golden State Killer (GSK). 'In the Footsteps of a Killer' also landed Michelle a book deal with HarperCollins.

In summer 2015, Paul moved to LA and became Michelle's lead researcher as she juggled being a mum, writing her book and continuing her ongoing crusade to uncover the Golden State Killer. While Michelle interviewed surviving rape victims and detectives who'd hunted the GSK, Paul continued his meticulous data mining, using geographic profiling to try to establish where the suspect might live. He trawled through more yearbooks to eliminate suspects based on the physical appearance of the GSK. Through her research, Michelle had established that the killer was built like a runner or swimmer, lean with 'big, muscular calves'. The GSK's blood type was A and he was a non-secretor (an individual whose blood type cannot be identified from antigens in other bodily fluids such as semen and saliva). He wore US size nine tennis shoes and was probably in his early twenties when the East Area rapes began. The GSK also had a 'conspicuously small penis,' she wrote on her blog.

Paul studied the varying police sketches of the suspect. Some drawings depicted a narrow-faced man with collar-length hair, whereas others illustrated a plump visage topped with a short back and sides, Hitleresque cut. Eyewitnesses claimed the serial rapist had sandy hair and hazel or blue eyes. His estimated height was a key factor, as Paul explains: 'Height is a very useful piece of information. Often, a person's height, weight and eye colour are included in court documents. We knew the GSK was probably between five-seven and five-eleven. So if I saw a person who was head and shoulders above their peers in a yearbook photo, I could eliminate that person just on this basis.'

Each time a suspect of interest cropped up, Paul added it to his burgeoning 'master list' – a document, complete with an index and photographs, containing the names and personal information of thousands of men. 'Throughout the investigation I studied over 100,000, maybe 200,000 names – but I recorded just a few thousand. It was very time-consuming, and I acknowledge that was probably why law enforcement had not thoroughly mined that reservoir.'

Paul then created a separate master file documenting over a million names of people who lived in Sacramento County in the mid to late seventies. 'I created a separate document for Orange County, South California, listing those who lived there in the early eighties. I ran a tool that compared the two lists then created a third document, adding the names of people who appeared in both counties.

'There are resources that can automate the process to a certain extent and – as Michelle and I got deeper into it – we started using those tools. For example, we had a utility that scraped the Sacramento County property records, which included millions of entries of grants and deeds. We then created another file for the scraped material.

'Of course, there were a lot of false positives; there were a lot of John A. Smiths and David Taylors out there, but there are some names that were more unique. If someone looked of interest, I would work on creating as much info on that person as I could.'

It's mind-boggling to assimilate the extensive range of resources and technology he and Michelle employed in their relentless endeavours to put a face to the GSK. 'Have you heard of OCR?' he asks with lifted brows. I mirror Paul's look and urge him to enlighten me. Apparently, OCR is an abbreviation for Optical Character Recognition – software that scans and analyses high volumes of text. 'I would do this with phone books or reverse directories,' Paul tells me, then pinches the bridge of his nose as he remembers the pitfalls of the software. 'Of course, it's very messy with errors and errant punctuation marks. The scanner would interpret a fleck of dirt on a page as an apostrophe. So, we had to apply additional processes to the scanned material to clean it up.'

I'm keen to hear about the people Paul and Michelle identified – and whether any of the names in their lists jumped out as a possible suspect? 'Sure, but there were red herrings and the more that happens the more desensitised one tends to grow towards returns like that. The returns were diminishing. It had been a while since my last discovery. Then, we borrowed the Mother Lode. I remember Michelle's source saying, before we made off with the documents, "I think the killer's identity is somewhere in Visalia. I hope you're looking into this angle?" We were sure we would find the GSK somewhere in those files.'

Paul and Michelle did find a possible suspect – and Michelle forwarded that name to Paul Holes, who was then working as a cold-case investigator for the Contra Costa County District Attorney's Office. Holes had been working on the GSK case with Michelle since before her *LA Magazine* article was published and the pair had developed an unbreakable professional bond. Unfortunately, the name Paul and Michelle flagged transpired not to be a viable suspect. So, their search continued − day and night, sifting through the Mother Lode and microscopically examining every possible lead.

Michelle came to believe that DNA profiling held the key to solving the interminable puzzle. By uploading the GSK's genetic profile into GEDmatch, a commercial database where people can enter their DNA from other genetic testing companies, they would be able to trace the killer's relatives − parents, siblings, half-siblings, first to fourth cousins even.

Sadly, Michelle would never witness a genetic breakthrough. A nocturnal existence began to take its toll on the sleuth, who was also trying to finish her book chronicling her exhaustive search for the GSK. She suffered from insomnia and often depended on drugs like Xanax to help her sleep.

Paul recalls the evening of 20 April, 2016, when he typed a long email to Michelle outlining his thoughts on a Mother Lode file she'd shared with him. 'She didn't reply, which wasn't entirely unusual − I knew she was busy. But when I hadn't heard from her by mid-afternoon the next day, I suspected I might have rubbed her the wrong way − because that's where my mind goes oftentimes when I don't hear back from people. Then I received an email from a close friend of Michelle, which seemed odd as I'd only met this friend twice. The email was short and worrying: "Hi Paul, please call me, it's very urgent." My heart dropped.'

Paul called Michelle's friend. Her friend's husband answered, his voice low and trembling. 'I'm sorry,' he said. 'It's Michelle. She passed away this morning.'

'I froze. I immediately went numb,' says Paul. Michelle was my mentor – and something of a maternal figure to me. I'd never had a healthy mother figure in my life, so I tend to seek this in other people. I loved working with Michelle; I had a lot of self-consciousness around my interest in the GSK, but with Michelle, I could speak endlessly about the case. And now, she was gone. I couldn't believe it. I knew she had a full plate – being a mother and author and citizen detective – but Michelle seemed to juggle all of this with a supernatural level of grace. Nothing had ever raised a red flag for me. Michelle's death came as a complete shock.'

Michelle McNamara died suddenly in her sleep at home, a week after her forty-sixth birthday. A coroner ruled that her death was caused by an accidental overdose of multiple prescription drugs, combined with a previously undiagnosed heart condition. She left behind 3,500 files related to the GSK case and her unfinished book, *I'll Be Gone in the Dark: One Woman's Obsessive Search for the Golden State Killer*.

The haunting title is a direct quote from the murderer, as told to Michelle by one of his surviving rape victims. Kris Pedretti, also known as victim number ten, had skipped a high-school dance and was alone in her family's house, playing the piano when the killer broke in and crept up behind her. Pressing the cold blade of his butcher's knife against her throat, he'd sneered, 'Get moving. If you say anything or flinch, I'll push the knife all the way in. You'll be silent for ever and I'll be gone in the dark of night.' He repeated this chilling phrase several times as he raped the fifteen-year-old girl on 18 December, 1976.

Michelle had gained the trust of several GSK rape victims. A victim herself – she was sexually assaulted by a man while studying in Belfast in 1992 – she shared a strong emotional bond with these women. Above all, she wanted justice for them. Her husband Patton poignantly said, following her unexpected death: 'Michelle listened with patience and heart to every story, no matter how deep the wound it described.'

Although bereft at losing his investigating partner, Paul could not let Michelle's search for justice remain unfinished. 'Michelle had put her whole being into the GSK case. It seemed only fitting to continue this work – for Michelle.' A week after her death, Paul teamed up with citizen sleuth and investigative journalist Billy Jenson and, together, they delved into the 3,500 files found on Michelle's hard drive. They leafed through stacks of her notepads and thousands of pages of digitised police reports and, of course, the contents of the Mother Lode.

'Michelle's files included notes to herself – stuff like, "Complete the reverse directory of Goleta residents," and "Figure out way to submit GSK's DNA to 23andMe or Ancestory.com." We found old maps of Goleta and photographs of bindings found at the GSK's crime scenes. There were pictures of the soles of shoes, which she'd compared to photographs of footprints left at the GSK's crime scenes, and a bulging folder about the Visalia Ransacker and theories she was developing to connect him to the rapes and murders of GSK. There were lists of potential suspects. We re-examined her every lead.'

Alongside sifting through the thousands of files and notes, Paul, Billy and Patton worked together to complete Michelle's book. Reading Michelle's manuscript, which Paul estimates was around 60 per cent finished, the men knew instantly they could not mimic Michelle's unique voice and arresting prose. 'Picking up the book was a challenge,' says Paul who, with Billy, wrote part three of the manuscript. 'Michelle's writing was incredible. Her book read much like Truman Capote's *In Cold Blood* – vivid yet sensitive and sympathetic towards the GSK's victims. We couldn't match Michelle's writing style – and we wouldn't try to. So, Billy and I worked through Michelle's notes to piece together the blanks. *I'll Be Gone in the Dark* was Michelle's legacy, and I felt honoured to contribute towards getting her work out there.'

I'll Be Gone in the Dark: One Woman's Obsessive Search for the Golden State Killer was published by HarperCollins in February 2018. At that moment the GSK's identity was still unknown. The book became a bestseller. Paul was also co-executive producer of the docuseries of the same title, which premiered on HBO in 2020.

Among the files on Michelle's hard drive that made it into the final manuscript of the book, was an open letter she wrote to the GSK. In a piece titled 'Letter to an Old Man', Michelle envisions the day of the GSK's capture. She imagines him hearing his doorbell ring and realising that justice has finally come for him and that he cannot escape into the night as he has before. The letter concludes: 'No side gates are left open. You're long past leaping over a fence. Take one of your hyper, gulping breaths. Clench your teeth. Inch timidly toward the insistent bell.

'This is how it ends for you. "You'll be silent forever, and I'll be gone in the dark," you threatened once.

'Open the door. Show us your face. Walk into the light.'

6

Snaring the Golden State Killer

Paul Haynes was promoting Michelle's book in Chicago when he heard that the Golden State Killer had been identified and arrested.

Mike Morford, a fellow true crime writer and host of the *Criminology* podcast phoned Paul with the news on that evening in April 2018. 'I was in my hotel room, trying to sleep, when Mike called,' Paul remembers. 'Patton, Billy Jenson and I had just done a panel session to promote Michelle's book and my mind was whirring with thoughts about the GSK. I hadn't slept the night before and I had the jitters from drinking endless cups of coffee. Then Mike called me.

'He said he'd spoken with one of my contacts, who'd heard the GSK had been identified and arrested. He said, "Y'know, Paul, we don't have a lot of information at this point, we don't have a name for him, so let's take this with a grain of salt for now." I agreed with Mike. After all, we'd encountered so many red herrings in this case . . . But, the GSK, captured? My thoughts instantly turned to Michelle.'

Another sleepless night followed for Paul. Into the early hours he mentally searched the Mother Lode and the lists of potential suspects he and Michelle had identified but not yet ruled out. He called and texted his contacts – and one confirmed that the news was true. After forty-three years police had finally caught the Golden State Killer. They'd knocked on his door and, when he answered, they'd seen his unmasked face in the light as Michelle had predicted. Her piece, 'Letter to an Old Man', played in Paul's head and his throat bulged with a concoction of elation and sadness. *'This is how it ends for you. Open the door. Show us your face. Walk into the light. Walk into the light. Walk into the light.'* Paul drifted into a short, fragmented sleep that ended when a flurry of pings came from his mobile phone. Messages from friends, sources, interview requests from media organisations had flooded in. And more information.

'The GSK is a seventy-two-year-old ex-cop,' one contact told Paul in a text. 'He was arrested in Sacramento County. No name for him yet but will keep you posted.'

'As soon as I saw the word "cop" my heart began to race,' says Paul. 'I'd run checks on numerous former police officers during my investigations, as Michelle and I had long thought the suspect might be from a law enforcement or military background. I was itching to make some calls to find out his name – I knew one of my sources would know this information by now, but I was running late. I had to get to the airport to catch my flight back to LA.'

By the time Paul's taxi to the airport arrived, he knew the identity of the GSK. His name was Joseph DeAngelo: a dad, a grandfather, a former police officer and – to the neighbours he'd fooled for so many years – 'just an ordinary Joe'. His mugshot revealed a scowling old man; a bald head splodged with liver spots, broken veins meshed on his broad saggy jowls, a humped chin, ears like battered moccasins and an evil flare in his piggish blue-grey eyes.

Joseph DeAngelo had not crossed Paul's radar until now. Reading the news on his phone, he longed to call Michelle. 'I remember scrolling through reports on my way to the airport, looking for any piece of information I could find on Joseph DeAngelo. I didn't recognise his name as one that had appeared on my many lists. There was a mugshot of DeAngelo online. And many pictures of Michelle kept cropping up on the newsfeed. And that really undercut the excitement for me because Michelle had not lived to see the fruit of her unfinished work – or get the answers she'd sought. That was bittersweet.'

A covert investigation involving genetic genealogy had led to DeAngelo's identification and capture. In 2018, cold-case investigator and friend of Michelle, Paul Holes, had enlisted the help of a crime lab to identify the full DNA profile of the Golden State Killer. This was extracted from semen samples obtained from his victims' rape kits. Just as Michelle had suggested during her research into the crime series, Holes uploaded the killer's DNA profile to GEDmatch. Thousands of hours of research followed the results from the upload to GEDmatch, with around twenty potential third or fourth cousins of the GSK identified in a family tree dating back to the 1800s.

As Holes continued to work through his list of potential suspects – over 8,000 were being considered prior to analysis of the preserved semen sample – the genealogist Barbara Rae-Venter contacted him with a lead. She had found a newspaper article from 3 October, 1979, concerning a police officer in Auburn, California, who had been kicked out of the force for shoplifting. Officer Joseph DeAngelo was caught stealing a can of dog repellent and a hammer from a local drugstore. 'Have you ruled out Joseph DeAngelo?' Barbara asked in her email to Holes.

DeAngelo was indeed on Holes' list, which he'd now narrowed down to six likely suspects. Uploading the GSK's DNA profile to another system, Barbara confirmed that the suspect would be blue-eyed and prematurely bald. Law enforcement then pulled California drivers' records for the remaining suspects – and only one had blue eyes: Joseph DeAngelo.

Finally, Holes and Barbara had found their prime suspect. DeAngelo matched the right age group and had lived in the same areas of California where the crime sprees occurred. And photographs of DeAngelo in his late twenties bore striking similarities to the police sketches drawn from survivor and witness descriptions of the GSK.

Convinced they'd found the man, investigators staked out DeAngelo's home that he shared with his daughter and granddaughter: a three-bedroom ranch house in Citrus Heights, Sacramento County – he truly had hidden in plain sight right there in California and for more than four decades. They needed definitive proof that DeAngelo was their man. When no one was home, undercover officers fished a dirty tissue out of DeAngelo's rubbish bin. Holes then plugged the DNA extracted from the discarded tissue into the genealogy database and found that it matched the profile of the GSK.

DeAngelo was arrested on his driveway on 24 April, 2018. When police raided his home, they found trinkets in his bedroom including cufflinks, necklaces and heart pendants – trophies he had stolen from his helpless victims.

In June 2020, DeAngelo pleaded guilty to thirteen counts of first-degree murder and multiple kidnapping charges. In a plea bargain that spared him the death penalty, the Golden State Killer admitted other uncharged offences, including nearly fifty rapes and more than 120 burglaries, mostly in Sacramento, the eastern San Francisco Bay area and Southern California.

At his sentencing hearing two months later, DeAngelo appeared in a wheelchair, playing the part of a frail old man dressed in his orange jumpsuit. He didn't know that prosecutors had secret footage filmed days earlier that showed the serial killer exercising and clambering over furniture in his jail cell.

Paul Haynes watched the televised proceedings from home. He would have gone to the hearing himself, but the coronavirus pandemic prevented him from doing so. As it occurred at the peak of the pandemic, DeAngelo's sentencing took place in a ballroom at Sacramento State University – a venue large enough for socially-distanced seating.

Watching from his home, Paul noticed how DeAngelo avoided eye contact with his brave rape victims. 'DeAngelo wouldn't look at his victims or anybody in the public gallery,' notes Paul. 'When committing his crimes, DeAngelo would often say to his victims, "Don't look at me." I think there was some core level of shame around what he was doing. After raping women, he would go off into corners and start sobbing. It's as if he was at war with himself – and still is – and so much time has passed since his last known crime that he's just put it out of his mind. He doesn't want to think about it. He is still a narcissistic individual.'

Over a dozen survivors of the GSK waived their anonymity to give powerful impact statements during the hearing. Watching DeAngelo's rape victims deliver their statements makes for difficult viewing – but, equally, it's empowering to see these women finally confront the man who struck insurmountable fear into their hearts. Their voices, wrought with decades-worth of trauma, matter.

One of the first victims to face the GSK at the hearing, was Mary Berwert. Her voice shuddered as she thanked those who'd helped put 'that man in the dock today', but Mary's expression was one of sheer determination as she glared at the monster who broke into her home and raped her, when she was just a little girl, in her bedroom. 'No thirteen-year-old should have to find out what a rape kit is,' said Mary.

At 4 a.m. on 25 June, 1979, DeAngelo, then a serving cop for Auburn City Police Department, had forced his way into the home Mary shared with her father and sister in Walnut Creek, California. Mary woke to the sound of breathing in her bedroom. The slow, steady breaths became louder, closer, and when Mary opened her eyes, a man in a ski mask loomed over her, forcing a knife against her throat. Before Mary could scream for help, DeAngelo stuffed a bra into her mouth and bound her wrists and ankles with twine. 'I will kill you and your family if you make a sound,' he said in what she remembers as an 'evil scratchy whisper.' Before raping Mary, he callously asked her, 'Have you ever had sex?'

Until that terrifying moment, Mary, had been enjoying an 'idyllic summer before starting eighth grade.' She'd recently gained a coveted place in a Walnut Creek cheerleading squad. Mary was a happy teenager with her whole life ahead of her. With his depraved, unthinkable act that night, DeAngelo robbed Mary of her happiness, dignity and innocence.

'Walnut Creek was a happy place. I had a happy life,' Mary said in her impact statement. 'Joseph DeAngelo forced his way into my home, into my life and into my room. A *child's* room. A room personally decorated with hand-painted hearts and rainbows and quotes about love and kindness on the walls. Unicorn mobiles hung from the ceiling.

'He raped me. He stole my innocence, my security. He threatened my life. He threatened the lives of my family. That night, after he raped me, I had to break the ties on my legs, thinking, "*Mind over matter, mind over matter. Mind. Over. Matter.*" I had to open my bedroom door with my hands tied behind my back, the whole time knowing I must go through my father's door and tell him what had happened. I ran to his door, with my hands still tied behind my back and cried, "Daddy, I've been raped."

'My dad flew out of his bed. He started crying. I'd never seen him cry before. He called the police, and I was taken to the hospital.

'My family couldn't hide the agony on their faces. When they looked at me, I knew that it wasn't my fault, but I also knew that the sight of me caused them pain. There are things you can't unsee.'

DeAngelo – wearing long-sleeved T-shirt over his jumpsuit, a surgical mask obscuring his mouth – remained impassive throughout Mary's statement, his cold, empty gaze fixated somewhere above his victim's head.

'The impact doesn't go away,' Mary continued. 'We live with it. It moves in and out of the blind spots. The rear-view mirror of our lives going forward. And it's always there.'

In the aftermath of the attack, Mary would sleep with the lights on as her trauma haunted her thoughts and dreams. 'I'd get out of bed, check the lock. Wake up every morning at 4 a.m., check the lock again and lay there and wait until daylight. When eighth grade began, I would get ready for school. I would get up early, at 4 a.m. As soon as I left the house a neon sign lit up my forehead. It said: "Raped." I couldn't turn it off, so I had to be brighter than that sign.

'When I went to school, I had to prove that I was no different than I had been before. Dad devoted more time to me. I was a cheerleader. He was a cheerleader's dad. He painted the house a different colour, changed the landscaping. He put extra security locks on the door, but nothing could fix it. I didn't feel safe there.'

During the year before he attacked Mary, DeAngelo had raped at least fifteen women, including Gay Hardwick. Her husband, Robert, who was also a victim of DeAngelo, stood beside his wife at the podium, head bowed, as she gave her statement. The couple were dating and had just bought their first house in Stockton, California when DeAngelo struck on 18 March, 1978. He broke into their new home, crept into the bedroom, and woke Gay and Robert by shining a flashlight into their eyes. At gunpoint, DeAngelo then tied them both up before blindfolding Gay and raping and sexually assaulting her for several hours.

'Joseph DeAngelo attacked us while we were sleeping,' Gay began. 'He kidnapped me from our bed. He raped me repeatedly. He sodomised me. He forced oral copulation. He stole the few precious pieces of jewellery that I owned, which were gold rings given to me by my brother and my parents to commemorate my graduation from college the year before. I was the first girl to graduate from college [in my family], so those pieces were special to me.'

After raping Gay, DeAngelo helped himself to food and beers from the couple's fridge while she lay 'blindfolded and unclothed on the cold, wood floor'.

'The door was open on that cold, March night. He ate from my fridge and drank two beers. He ransacked our home and tormented me with threats of death for me and my loved ones should I make a sound or resist in any way. The aftermath of this attack has been with me for forty-two years. That's a very long life sentence for somebody who had done nothing to deserve such hatred, violence and desecration of my body.'

Her husband, Robert, added to his wife's impact statement: 'Joseph DeAngelo appeared in our life. He broke into our home, tied me up at gunpoint. He sought and raped Gay repeatedly. It was terrifying for me because I was thoroughly helpless. I could do nothing to protect her. Gay was the victim of a horrible assault, and I was a victim because I would have to live for the rest of my life knowing I was helpless to prevent this attack.'

'We decided that we weren't going to let Mr DeAngelo, this gentleman sitting here,' – Robert gestured towards DeAngelo who, again, stared at the wall – 'define our lives. And we were not going to be cast aside because of this attack.

'The hardest thing for me over the years was my wife having panic attacks, knowing there was absolutely nothing I could do except to support her. I can't erase her traumas. Joseph DeAngelo is an animal of the worst kind. How the Lord could create such a human being, I do not know.'

Kris Pedretti – the victim who had relayed the quote 'I'll be gone in the dark' to Michelle McNamara – told how she sang a hymn in her head while 'waiting to die' when DeAngelo assaulted her when she was just fifteen years old. 'He stole my youth, my innocence. Who could I have grown up to be? I guess I'll never know. He tormented me. And he told me, over and over again, he would kill me, and I believed him. At three different times that night, I thought I was going to die. I sang "Jesus Loves Me" in my head as I waited to die. The next morning, I woke up knowing I would never be a child again and, although I was truly grateful to be alive, I also felt that I had died.'

In October 1976, Jane Carson-Sandler was at home with her three-year-old son when knife-wielding DeAngelo forced his way into the property and raped her. In keeping with his habitual modus operandi, DeAngelo bound, blindfolded and gagged Jane and her son, then threatened to kill them throughout a sustained attack that left Jane 'frozen with fear beyond description'.

Staring down at her rapist as she made her statement, Jane addressed DeAngelo as 'evil one' as she implored: 'I want you to look at me, Joseph James DeAngelo. I want you to look at me and I want you to remember, what I have to say. On 5 October, 1976, you broke into my home in the early hours, and you shoved your knife into my neck, you bound my wrists and ankles. You blindfolded me then gagged me with a cloth. But you also did the same to my precious three-year-old son. How *dare* you?

'A quarter of me, being a Christian, wants to say, may God have mercy on your soul. But there's another three quarters of me who just wants to tell you, buddy, to rot in hell.'

Following the survivors' statements, Judge Michael Bowman asked DeAngelo whether he wished to address the court. 'Mr DeAngelo would like to make a brief statement,' confirmed the killer's defence team.

The courtroom fell silent as DeAngelo rose, unaided and with ease, from his wheelchair and slowly unhooked his surgical mask from his ears. A look of confusion then swathed his face as he stared down at the face-covering hammocked between his hands. 'After . . . listening . . . to . . .' DeAngelo began, then momentarily closed his eyes, the tendons in his neck visibly straining as he gulped. '. . . all of your statements. Each one of them . . . And I'm truly sorry for everyone I've hurt.' DeAngelo spoke for only a few seconds, his unexpected mea culpa prompting sharp gasps from the public gallery. But for DeAngelo's victims, no apology could erase the deep-rooted agony he'd inflicted.

Judge Michael Bowman said he was 'moved' by the victims' 'courage, grace and strength.' Then, addressing DeAngelo, he added, 'All qualities you lack. Are you capable of comprehending the pain and anguish you've caused? You deserve no mercy.' Judge Bowman sentenced DeAngelo to life in prison without the possibility of parole. As security guards wheeled the Golden State Killer out of the ballroom, everyone in the room – prosecutors, those in the public gallery and his victims – rose as one in a round of applause.

When I ask Paul Haynes what he made of DeAngelo's 'apology', he pulls his head back, looking unconvinced. He's since replayed the clip numerous times, trying to decipher the deeper meaning behind DeAngelo's words. 'I watched his apology several times and, with each viewing, it resonated a little differently. In my opinion it was a narcissistic, self-serving apology. What I saw was basically, "Here's my contrition, are you happy?" I also questioned whether DeAngelo actually said sorry to those that he'd "hurt". To me, it sounded like he'd apologised to those that he'd "heard". But it's impossible to discern.

'I have so many questions I'd like to put to DeAngelo – one being, what happened with the Maggiores that led to their deaths? I've thought about writing to DeAngelo. I would like to visit him in jail, but I doubt he'll respond.'

DeAngelo's name didn't appear in Paul or Michelle's files and, after DeAngelo's arrest, authorities were quick to declare that Michelle's work chronicling the GSK case did 'not help with the apprehension of a suspect.'

Paul disagrees. 'Michelle did not invest her life's work in this case to seek glory. She cared about the GSK being brought to justice – and seeking answers for his victims. Her investigation might not have named the suspect in the end, but what Michelle did was to shine a light on a case that had stagnated. She made the case visible – and that brought DeAngelo into the light.'

7

Forever Young

Livingston, New York, June 2015

'I was fine until this one song came on the radio in the gas station minimart,' says Carl Koppelman, spreading his hands. 'I grabbed an iced tea from the refrigerator, headed towards the checkout and, wow, the opening chords of Rod Stewart's "Forever Young" flooded my ears and I just fell apart.

'Tears streamed down my face. The guy behind the checkout became a watery shape but I sensed he was giving me a strange look that asked, *"Why are you crying at Rod Stewart's 'Forever Young'?"* My eyes welled and spilled, welled and spilled. Constant, unstoppable tears shed – not for me, but for Tammy Jo Alexander, a sixteen-year-old girl found murdered in a field in 1979.

'I'd just attended Tammy Jo's memorial service, where her friend Alice had told me how the pair loved dancing to Rod Stewart's *Blondes Have More Fun* album. And I could picture that scene as I stood in the minimart, crying among those people going about their everyday lives, thinking, *"Tammy Jo will always be forever young"*.'

Carl Koppelman, an accountant by day, has an extraordinary yet incredible hobby: he creates digital illustrations of unnamed dead people, depicting how they would have looked when alive in the hope of identifying them and providing answers for their loved ones. And he did just that for the family and friends of Tammy Jo Alexander.

Until January 2015, Tammy was known as Caledonia Jane Doe, or Cali Doe for short. She was an unidentified homicide victim discovered in Caledonia, a small town in Livingston County, New York.

A farmer found the teenager's body dumped in a rain-lashed cornfield bordering Route 20 on the morning of 10 November, 1979. The victim was face down in the sodden earth and covered with dirt. A bullet had been fired into her back, puncturing the danger-red nylon jacket that bloated like a lifebuoy around her dead torso. She had on tan corduroy trousers, blue socks and brown ripple-soled shoes. The farmer gagged on wet air ripe with blood and death and stumbled no more than ten paces to the roadside – then he ran to a nearby diner to call the police.

Soon after, sheriff's deputies and police officers arrived at the desolate murder scene. They combed the cornfield and neighbouring land for miles, but their search, hampered by the overnight deluge, produced nothing that would lead them to the girl's killer.

Investigators did, however, find a spent slug from a .38 calibre handgun beneath the victim's body – and deduced that the murderer had shot Cali Doe at the roadside then dragged her into the cornfield. Further examination of the corpse revealed a second bullet wound just above the victim's right eye. Detectives believed the young woman had not turned or flinched when the bullet hit her head, suggesting she had been taken by surprise.

Cali Doe's pockets had been turned out. Attached to the belt loops on her trousers were two keychains. One was a heart with a keyhole, inscribed with the message: 'He who holds the key can open my heart.' The second trinket was the key to that metal heart. At the time, the keyrings were sold in vending machines at rest stops along the New York State Thruway. She also had on a necklace, threaded with silver beads and three turquoise stones, one resembling a bird.

The FBI had little evidence with which to work. Cali Doe's autopsy revealed she had eaten a meal of canned ham, sweetcorn and potatoes shortly before her death. Marge Bradford, then a waitress at a diner in Lima, told police that a young woman matching Cali Doe's description had eaten at the restaurant on the evening before her body was found. Marge said the girl had arrived around 8.30 p.m., accompanied by an older white man wearing a checked shirt and black wire-rimmed glasses. He had curly dark hair and had driven a tan station wagon, Marge told detectives and added, 'Why would you buy someone dinner – then kill them forty-five minutes later and throw them in a cornfield?' Police issued a composite sketch of the mystery man allegedly seen with Cali Doe, but no concrete leads materialised.

Meanwhile, the slug found at the death scene did not match any bullets from weapons confiscated in North America or Europe, and the torrential rainfall had washed away most forensic evidence. Officers could find no DNA on Cali Doe's clothing or body, but bikini or halter top tan lines crossing her shoulders and heart suggested the teen had travelled to New York from somewhere much balmier. Her molar teeth were riddled with cavities.

A handful of locals attended Cali Doe's small funeral at Mount Morris Cemetery in Dansville, New York. Her epitaph read: 'Lest we forget. Unidentified girl. Nov, 1979. And flights of angels sing thee to thy rest.'

Days, weeks, months, and then years passed. The FBI launched multiple media appeals and plastered posters on billboards across America, hoping that somebody might provide information that would unmask Cali Doe's killer or at least identify the tragic teen abandoned in the soggy dirt. But, despite being swamped with thousands of tips, police came no closer to solving the horrific case – and Cali Jane Doe's identity would remain a mystery for decades.

That was until Carl began working on a facial reconstruction from Cali Doe's autopsy photographs. But, before hearing how he helped give a name to the girl, gunned down a week after her sixteenth birthday, I'm keen to discover more about Carl's craft and the techniques he employs to visually resurrect the dead.

Unfortunately, a five-and-a-half thousand-mile transatlantic flight stops me from turning up at Carl's door in Torrance, California, so I instead settle for an online meeting with the self-taught forensic artist from my London bedroom. Now in his late fifties, Carl fits his sleuthing around a forty-hours-a-week job as a CPA accountant – often working late into the night creating portraits of the deceased. A prominent name in the amateur and professional crime-busting fraternities, Carl is also a moderator for Tricia Griffith at Websleuths.com (an online community of discussion forums dedicated to crime and missing and unidentified persons – see chapter 4). This is the community that inspired his venture into forensic artistry when he stumbled upon the site in August 2009.

He says, 'I was reading the news online one morning and a story caught my attention. It was about an eleven-year-old girl, Jaycee Lee Dugard, who was grabbed off a street in California in 1991 and held captive for eighteen years. Everybody thought Jaycee was dead but in 2009 police found her alive at her captors' home. Jaycee's abductors – Phillip and Nancy Garrido were arrested, and the girl was returned to her mother. By that time, Jaycee was twenty-nine-years-old.

'I began researching the story online and that's how I discovered Websleuths.com. I had never heard of this community before. There were so many people working on cases involving unidentified bodies – and doing so from their homes. I found this fascinating and thought, "*Hey, maybe this is something I could do?*"'

Back then, Carl had taken a break from work to look after his ailing mother, Shirley Merrill, at her home in El Segundo, California. 'I discovered that helping to identify unnamed dead people was something I could do from my home computer between caring for my mother,' he explains. 'I never realised there were so many unidentified people and helping to give those victims names seemed, to me, a worthwhile thing to do. Some forensic portraits I'd seen of Jane and John Does did not appear very accurate and, because I have artistic abilities, I thought I'd try creating some portraits myself.

'As my mother's caretaker, I was restricted to the house, which gave me lots of time to work on my computer. My portraits were well received and soon I was inundated with requests to recreate images for John and Jane Does – and missing people too.

'When my mother passed away in 2017, I had to return to my day job, but I still work as a forensic artist in my spare time. My whole objective is to create portraits that are visually appealing – to draw eyes to the images so that people will engage with the stories and share them on social media.'

I wonder how the disparate skills of balancing books and painting interconnect, but according to Carl, the two talents complement each other perfectly. 'I developed my art skills when I was young, so I've always been good at drawing. But being a CPA accountant requires good analytical skills, and that analytical nature in me is useful when creating my digital reconstructions – plus I'm great at spreadsheets, which I use to keep track of the Does and missing people.'

Typing 'Carl Koppelman' into Google images renders dozens of faces of the dead brought to life by the accountant. Many of his reconstructions have led to the identification of John and Jane Does. Once the victims are identified, the likenesses Carl captures are revealed to be phenomenal. Unlike some of the black-and-white police sketches out there, his portraits resemble photographic-style oil paintings. They're tangible. The faces have character, with soulful eyes, contours, and varying skin tones. They frown or smile or scowl or raise their brows in surprise – expressions Carl matches according to the anatomy of the remains in the autopsy picture from which he's working. Often, those cadavers are badly decomposed or disfigured from brutal force. When a victim is found face down, like Cali Jane Doe for example, blood flows to the surface of the skin, causing severe redness and swelling, Carl tells me. Other times, the remains consist of only a skull.

Carl gives life to his subjects via the medium of Corel Photo-Paint, a digital photo-editing package with a host of realistic special effects, from retouching to photo-painting.

'Corel Photo-Paint is kind of like Adobe Photoshop. It's a very high-quality graphics programme that I use as though I'm painting on canvas. I begin by searching online for a model who I think might resemble the remains. Then I take that photograph, make it 90 to 95 per cent transparent, and superimpose the image on the picture of the deceased person. The effect is such that the colour and vitality of that person shines through on the remains without the structural elements of the living person showing.

'I'll take up to ten pictures of studio models of similar age, sex, gender, and race as the victim and layer those images upon the coroner's photograph. This gives me a depiction of what the dead person might have looked like alive. Then I'll use other techniques to provide skin and muscle tone and, where possible, recreate the person's original hairstyle.'

Once he's established a fitting skin tone, Carl then uses lighting and shading techniques to sculpt the contours of the victim's face. Attention to detail at this stage is paramount. 'Get the brow line wrong, and you won't get a good likeness,' Carl tells me. However, achieving an authentic representation depends upon the information available in each case. 'Obviously, the more I know about the Doe's physical description, the better,' explains Carl. The quality of the autopsy picture is a big factor, too. Some victims look as though they're sleeping but others are quite badly decomposed, which makes the process more challenging.

'When I'm working from an image of a skull, I examine the shape and breadth of the cheekbones. Brow structure and the space between eyes are also key components for getting a good likeness, as are the mouth and chin. By using light and shadow I can create contours that conform to the bone structure of the skull. In some cases, if a skull has a unique teeth alignment or a crowned tooth, these characteristics will be displayed in the coroner's photograph.

'Looking at a skull probably doesn't a have a whole lot of meaning to most people who don't have an eye for this. But it is very helpful for me. I can probably come up with something to spur someone's memory to say, "Oh, that looks approximately like someone I remember."'

Carl sources some of the post-mortem photographs he reconstructs from the public database, NamUs, but, nowadays, coroners frequently approach him directly with images they want him to work on.

Skeletal remains cases are the most challenging, says Carl. 'I've just completed a depiction based entirely on a skull. I had no information on the man's hair or anything – just that he was middle-aged. My solution was to put a watch cap (woollen beanie-style hat) on him. He was found in Minnesota in the winter, so I thought – OK, that's a cold climate, he could have been wearing a hat.'

To date, Carl has worked on over three hundred portraits but claims his depiction of Cali Jane Doe was the image that earned him his reputation in the field of forensic artistry. He picked up the case in 2010, five years after authorities exhumed Cali Jane Doe's remains to obtain DNA from her bones and hair after advances in forensic technology.

In 2006, forensic palynologists examined the young woman's clothing. Using the science of Palynology (the study of spores and pollen grains), they analysed the pollen found on Cali Doe's clothes, and experts matched the particles to trees in Florida, Arizona and Southern California. This suggested she may have visited those regions before coming to New York.

Equipped with this forensic evidence and a copy of Cali Doe's autopsy photograph, Carl entirely threw himself into recreating her features with his artwork, determined to identify the girl who had been found in the cornfield.

The autopsy photographs of Cali Doe make for harrowing viewing. One picture shows the victim with her head rolled to the right, her young complexion like white wax. Brown hair, strewn with blonde frosting, hugs the nape of her neck in matted clumps. She has a dainty Tinker Bell nose, round cheeks and her lips are slightly parted. In the picture, Cali Doe's eyes are closed.

Carl was still getting to grips with the digital software when he painted his first version of Cali Doe. 'Back then I had a poor understanding of how the graphics worked,' he admits, 'so I made very few alterations to the post-mortem photo. I just opened her eyes – which I knew to be brown – straightened her hair a bit, and created an outfit for her that resembled the clothing she was found in. Her skin still had the pasty look of a deceased person. I continued to revise my reconstruction of Cali Doe as my competency with the software improved – and that's when I discovered the superimposing technique.'

Cali Doe's features became a permanent image in Carl's mind. He could visualise the shapes her lips and cheeks made in the days when she spoke, smiled, laughed and cried. 'I knew her face so well I would recognise her in a photograph immediately,' he says, swaying his head a little. 'Likewise, I was hoping somebody out there, a relative or friend, would recognise this girl from my drawing.'

Carl's final portrait captured a pretty teenager with a heart-shaped face, smoky quartz eyes, a pert nose and peachy lips curling into a faint smile that exposed her front teeth. She has chin-length hair, parted in the middle and set in a feathery pixie-style. She wears a turquoise and silver beaded necklace around her throat.

Carl posted his rendering on Websleuths and NamUs, but his campaign to identify the girl in the post-mortem photo did not end there. Intrigued by the pollen evidence the indefatigable sleuth sifted through late 1970s high school yearbooks from Florida, Arizona and Southern California. While caring for his mother, Carl spent hours upon hours trawling the pages of Classmates.com, which holds digital copies of the annual publications. He studied hundreds of black-and-white pictures of female students, zooming in on faces aglow with happiness and hope and enlarging mouths that could smile no wider. He would scrutinise browbones, cheekbones, eyes, lips and hair – looking for the cute Tinker Bell nose perched upon the now-familiar heart-shaped face that flashed continually, like an animated billboard, in Carl's head.

At one point, Carl thought he'd found Cali Doe among the serried parade of smiles. A visage jumped out at him with a convincing resemblance to his portrait. He tracked the girl from the photograph down in Ohio. 'But,' Carl remembers, although his cheeks still rise as he smiles at the recollection, 'turned out she was alive and working in a bookstore.' He found two more women who bore a similar likeness to Cali Doe – one in Minnesota, the other in San Diego – and both answered the phone when Carl called.

Carl shared theories with fellow Websleuthers in a thread dedicated to the Cali Doe mystery. The group eliminated some missing teenage girls as possible identifications for Cali Doe through their research. But, as more potential names were crossed off the list, another possible theory became more likely. Cali Doe could have run away from home. 'This was a concern,' explains Carl. 'If a child was assumed a runaway in the seventies, that child's missing person file would be purged when he or she turned eighteen. So, even if Cali Doe *had* been reported missing by her family, if she were designated as a runaway there would be no surviving record of them doing so.' Were Cali Doe's relatives even alive now? There were so many unanswered questions

Over the next four years Carl continued to tweak Cali Doe's portrait and digitally thumb through yearbook pages searching for her face. Every day he returned to his desk and scoured missing person profiles, looking for new entries in Florida, South California and Arizona. It wasn't unusual for Carl to spend up to twelve hours a day in front of his monitor, willing the face of the real Cali Doe to make herself known.

Scrolling through NamUs's gallery one Wednesday evening in September 2014, Carl remembered the inscription on Cali Doe's headstone and was struck with a thought: '*She deserves a name. Nobody should go to their grave unidentified.*' Profiles shunted up the screen. Then, at once, a face he knew well but had not seen before on NameUs appeared 'like a ghost.' His heart jumped. He felt his skin warm and tighten. '*I think this could be her,*' he thought, enlarging the picture of the girl who could have been a model for an American teenage magazine. She had rich brown eyes and an upturned nose. Fawn hair, highlighted blonde, bounced in curly crests about her temples, cheeks and chin. Her skin held a light tan and, as for the girl's smile . . . It radiated the sweetness of youth. '*It* must *be her.*'

The girl in the picture was Tammy Jo Alexander, born on 2 November, 1963, in Atlanta, Georgia. She had last lived in the city of Brooksville, in Hernando County, Florida. It was from here that she disappeared sometime between 1977 and 1979, the NamUs report confirmed.

'I was shocked,' Carl recalls, 'kind of excited but also sad. I was pretty sure Tammy Jo Alexander was Cali Doe as she certainly bore a strong resemblance to my rendition. But I'd only seen Cali Doe dead – and here was Tammy Jo, alive and smiling. It was like seeing a ghost.

'I made Tammy Jo's photograph 95 per cent transparent and superimposed it onto Cali Doe's autopsy picture. It matched perfectly. Even her bite lined up.'

He was so familiar with her face that Carl had long maintained that he 'would recognise her in a photograph immediately.' And now, he was convinced that long-awaited moment had arrived. He couldn't wait to share his find on the Websleuths' Cali Doe forum. Carl's message, number 1,494 in the thread, is still on the message board today. Posted at 9.21 p.m. on 24 September, 2014, it reads, 'BINGO!' Side by side below the red text sits the vibrant high school picture of Tammy Jo Alexander and Carl's portrait rendered from post-mortem photographs. Five words complete Carl's post: 'I think this is Cali!!!' His Websleuths comrades agreed, filling the board with congratulatory messages.

'Dang, Carl!! This is HUGE! Jawdrop,' wrote a member who goes by the username 'annemc2'.

EmiLove832 commented: 'Wow!! That has to be her!! Awesome find, Carl!'

'This brings tears to my eyes; this poor girl is finally going to get her name back, and maybe whoever killed her will be caught. Great job Carl,' posted another Websleuther.

Carl emailed the pictures to Livingston County Sheriff's office in New York, the Hernando County Sheriff's Office in Florida, NamUs and the National Center for Missing and Exploited Children. 'I think they are the same person,' he wrote in the accompanying email.

Police in both states acted swiftly to track down any existing relatives of Tammy Jo. It then transpired that she may never have been reported missing at all were it not for a former high school friend.

In the summer of 2013, Laurel Nowell found herself wondering what had become of a girl she'd known as a child, Tammy Jo, so she embarked on a mission to reconnect with her childhood pal with the 'big smile'. Nowell had moved away after high school and the pair had lost touch. Laurel joined Facebook, hoping to find Tammy Jo's profile. Unaware she had vanished without trace thirty-four years ago, Laurel couldn't find her friend. Further internet searches led her to the obituary for Tammy Jo's mother, Barbara Jenkins, who passed away in 1998 aged fifty-six. Barbara's death notice also listed Tammy Jo as deceased but mentioned that Barbara was survived by another daughter, Pamela Dyson, Tammy Jo's younger half-sister. Laurel was confused; she could find no official record of her friend's death. She did, however, manage to trace Pamela, who was living in Panama City.

The mystery deepened. Pamela told Laurel she'd gone to live with her grandmother when she was eleven and had subsequently lost touch with her sister. As far as Pamela knew, Tammy Jo had disappeared in 1979, and she thought their mother had reported her missing to police. Pamela hoped her sibling, who frequently ran away from home, had simply escaped a 'toxic family environment.' In August 2014, the two women filed a fresh missing person report for Tammy Jo with the Hernando County Sheriff's Office. Police told Pamela and Laurel they could find no evidence suggesting Tammy Jo's relatives reported her missing in 1979.

Following Carl's tip that Tammy Jo could be Cali Doe, investigators approached Pamela Dyson for a DNA sample to compare with the one extracted from the murder victim's exhumed remains. Mitochondrial DNA analysis confirmed the two samples to be a positive match. On 26 January, 2015, law enforcement officials in Livingston County, New York, announced that the girl found slain in a cornfield thirty-five years previously, had finally been identified as Tammy Jo Alexander.

'That was a pretty big moment,' says Carl, 'and while I was pleased to have played a part in identifying Cali Doe, it pained me to think of the brutal way her young life ended. How could somebody kill a young woman and abandon her in a cornfield?

'I realised Tammy Jo would have been just shy of a year younger than me – had she lived – and as I spoke to her friends and relatives, I began to discover more about the kind of girl she was. Tammy Jo came from a turbulent home, yet she was known as a bubbly, outgoing girl who enjoyed life.'

Tammy Jo didn't really know her biological father, Joe Alexander, who has also since passed away. She lived with her stepfather, Lloyd Jenkins and mother, Barbara, who was addicted to prescription medication and would fly into violent rages. Barbara had, on occasion, slit her wrists in front of a young Tammy Jo. During a January 2015 interview with *USA*

Today, Pamela Dyson recalled of her mother: 'She was suicidal. I think she had issues back then that they didn't diagnose. My mother put Joan Crawford to shame.' As a child, Tammy Jo spent time in foster homes and lived with her grandmother for a while.

Barbara and Lloyd owned L&M Truck Stop in Brooksville, located on Route 98. Before her disappearance, Tammy Jo waitressed with her mum at the rest stop's restaurant and was known to have run away on numerous occasions. She would hitchhike with truckers to flee the area. Once, she and Laurel hitchhiked from Florida to California. On that occasion, Carl points out that Barbara made no effort to find her runaway daughter. 'When the two girls arrived in California, Laurel called her parents from a payphone. They were desperately worried and immediately paid for airline tickets to fly Laurel and Tammy Jo back to Brooksville. But Tammy Jo's mother's reaction when she discovered where her daughter had ended up was to say, "Just leave her there." Which is very telling of the kind of mother she was.'

Other former high school friends of Tammy Jo remembered her for her infectious personality and go-getting attitude. Like most teenage girls, she had hopes and dreams. In Brooksville, Tammy Jo had a boyfriend, Kevin Williams, whom she planned to marry. One friend told Carl, 'Tammy Jo was in the Future Leaders of America at high school. She had talked of going to the University of Florida and planned to marry Kevin when she turned eighteen. She was very outgoing – not a shy bone in her. She loved chatting with truckers on the CB radio.'

By March 2015, the Livingston County Sheriff's Department announced it was pursuing new leads to find Tammy Jo's killer. Following tens of thousands of tips from the public, information concerning the teenager's whereabouts shortly before her death had come to light. Investigators had linked Tammy Jo to the former Rainbow Prison Ministry that nestled in a remote mountainous spot in Young Harris, Georgia. The organisation advised people on probation or parole. Police identified three men of interest connected to Tammy Jo, but DNA testing later ruled them out as suspects.

The murder of Tammy Jo Alexander remains unsolved today. The FBI is offering a reward of up to $20,000 for information leading to the arrest and conviction of her killer.

* * *

On 10 June, 2015, Carl attended a memorial service for Tammy Jo. Before this, he visited the scene of her murder. A photograph captures him standing at the edge of the field, clasping a printout displaying Tammy Jo's angelic face alongside his Cali Doe reconstruction. Route 20, tired, cracked and trafficless, disappears in a lonely grey swish beyond the horizon. The sky is a bleached duck-egg blue sheet, and a pond freshly filled with the previous night's rainfall shines silver in the morning sun. This is the place in the cornfield where Tammy Jo met her tragic fate.

'I felt I needed to see for myself the spot where this horrendous crime took place,' recalls Carl. 'Being there felt surreal because, until that point, I'd only seen photographs of the murder scene. I've always found it kind of easy to distance myself from the brutality of such crimes when sat behind my computer at home. But, standing in that cornfield, it hit home to me – the horrific reality of what happened there thirty-five years ago.'

Later that day, Carl joined Tammy Jo's relatives and friends at a moving service held in Greenmount Cemetery in Dansville. Pamela decided her sister should remain in her original resting place, among the people of Livingston County who had adopted and cared for Tammy Jo for almost four decades. The gravestone that once read, 'Lest we forget. Unidentified girl,' was replaced with a smooth granite rock bearing Tammy Jo's high school photograph and her name, etched in capitals – never to be forgotten. Today, the cemetery is a paradisiacal garden with its even shamrock lawn ringed by leafy sunlit trees.

Unlike Cali Doe's modest and quiet burial in the frozen graveyard decades ago, over a hundred people attended Tammy Jo's memorial ceremony. Wreaths and sprays composed of daisies, fuchsia roses and tangerine calendulas swathed Tammy Jo's headstone. At the remembrance service, which was filmed by *Livingston County News*, Pamela paid a tearful tribute to her older sister who 'used her beautiful smile to hide her pain.'

'Tammy was outgoing and friendly, adventurous and perhaps a little mischievous,' she said. 'Nobody who saw her could ever guess that she lived in a home where she was subjected to constant abuse. That is why she was a frequent runaway. That was her escape and safety net. Tammy Jo was a sweet and gentle person. Why would anybody murder her and throw her away? I'll never understand how anybody could look into her beautiful eyes and take her life in such a vicious way.'

Former Livingston County Sheriff, John York, also spoke at the ceremony. Addressing Pamela, he vowed the FBI would never stop looking for Tammy Jo's killer. 'Over ten thousand leads have been investigated as a result of the death of your sister. We'll bring an answer to you.' John thanked Laurel Nowell for reporting Tammy Jo missing and praised Carl's work. 'Carl Koppelman, we'll *never* forget the call that you made,' he said.

After the service, Carl decided to take a drive out to Letchworth State Park, a stunning attraction known locally as 'Grand Canyon East', where the Genesee River powers through a deep gorge. En route, he stopped at the gas station in Nunda, a small town about fourteen miles west of Dansville. He strolled across the forecourt, into the minimart and made a beeline for the refrigerator where he grabbed an iced tea. The air con nipped the back of his neck then frosted his spine as Rod Stewart's voice rasped over the radio. And that's when the tidal wave of emotion flooded Carl's entire being.

'As soon as "Forever Young" started playing I lost all control,' says Carl. 'Tammy Jo was a huge Rod Stewart fan. I thought about Tammy Jo and how she had been killed just one week after her sixteenth birthday. Again, I pictured her face – a face that had been with me for the last five years and, yeah, I just burst into tears then.

'I don't ordinarily get emotional about these things. As I said, I'm usually dealing with photographs – it's a mechanical process. But sometimes, my work results in a resolution in a case. And when I meet family members – and see how they've been affected by the whole thing – I do get emotional.'

Carl gravitates towards cases involving unidentified or missing teenagers and young adults. 'I guess they are a more sympathetic demographic,' he states. 'I'll always remember the news conference where Jaycee Dugard's mother, Terry Probyn, sobbed as she begged her daughter's abductors to release her girl. That stuck with me. Whenever I'm dealing with a case involving a young victim, I think about the mother who's praying for her child to come home.'

Carl has helped identify several children and young adults; he never gives up on a case, even when an investigation lingers on for years. One such case saw Carl team up with a woman called Cathy Terkanian from Gloucester, Massachusetts. The pair worked tirelessly together for ten years to find Cathy's missing daughter whom she'd been forced to give up for adoption thirty-six years previously.

Cathy was just seventeen when she gave birth in June 1974. She named her daughter Alexis but, with no support from family or authorities, Cathy reluctantly relinquished her rights as a mother. Alexis was placed for a closed adoption at five months old and was gone before her second birthday. Not a day passed that Cathy didn't think about her precious child. She had no idea who Alexis's new parents were but hoped they were caring and loving and providing the best life imaginable for her girl.

Then, in 2010, social services got in touch to inform Cathy that her daughter had gone missing from her home in Hamilton, Michigan, in March 1989. But the authorities would not reveal Alexis's adopted name. Heartbroken, Cathy turned internet detective and quickly found her daughter – now named Aundria Bowman – listed as missing on a Michigan police website. Cathy, recognised Aundria Bowman's face as she was one of the thirty-six images of missing children used in the 1993 'Runaway Train' music video by US indie rock band, Soul Asylum.

Cathy needed answers and she contacted Carl for help. The pair made four trips to Michigan, where they posted flyers and interviewed residents and schoolfriends of Aundria. Some friends said Aundria had told them that her adoptive father, Dennis Bowman, had molested her. Further investigation revealed that Bowman, a former naval reservist, had attacked a nineteen-year-old woman after luring her into a forest in 1980. He had pleaded guilty to assault with intent to commit criminal sexual conduct after striking a deal with prosecutors.

Fearing Bowman had killed Aundria and buried her body, Cathy and Carl studied court documents relating to the assault case and pushed police to ramp up the investigation into Aundria's disappearance – a case originally labelled an 'endangered runaway' by officers.

After years of sleuthing, the duo's suspicions about Bowman became a devastating reality. In early 2020, Carl received a telephone call from Cathy. 'It was the news we'd been waiting ten years to hear,' he recalls. 'Cathy said investigators were searching Bowman's home in Hamilton. I was glued to the news from that point. Later that day, police announced skeletal remains had been found in a shallow grave covered with concrete. I called Cathy back and said, "They finally found her. We did it."'

At that time, Bowman was in jail after being charged with the 1980 rape and murder of twenty-five-year-old Kathleen Doyle in Norfolk, Virginia. The search of the home he'd shared with his wife, Brenda, in Monterey Township, Allegan County, had been ordered after he confessed to killing Aundria in his prison cell.

He had told investigators how he pushed his adoptive daughter down the stairs when she threatened to report that he'd molested her. Aundria had died as a result of the fall and Bowman then called police to say his adopted daughter had stolen $100 from him and had 'run away from home.' Bowman went on to describe in sickening detail how he cut off Aundria's legs with an axe so that her torso would fit into a barrel bin. He said he'd placed Aundria's body parts in rubbish bags, which he 'put out with the rest of the trash.' Bowman then buried the bin containing her torso in his garden and filled the grave with a 'thin layer of cement.' DNA tests confirmed the remains found in Allegan County belonged to Aundria.

In June 2020, Bowman received two life sentences after pleading guilty to raping and murdering Kathleen Doyle. Eighteen months later, Bowman pleaded no contest to second-degree murder for the killing of Aundria. In February 2022, Bowman – wearing grey-and-white-striped jail clothes and a Covid mask – appeared at Allegan County Circuit Court to hear his fate. Judge Margaret Zuzich Bakker became visibly emotional, labelling Bowman a 'dangerous man', as she sentenced the murderer to a further thirty-five to fifty years behind bars.

8

It Started with a Murder

'I grew up in Pompton Lakes in New Jersey, a small and seemingly crimeless town – until, one day, a young woman was bludgeoned to death in her apartment. It was tragic; the whole community was in shock. *A slaying, in Pompton Lakes?* I was just eleven when the murder happened, but it was one of those cases that stayed with me. From then on, I became hooked on true crime. I wanted to learn more about murders. So, I decided: *"I'm going to join the FBI when I leave school."'*

Tracie Boyle's black cat, Hollie, languidly slinks across the desk in front of her computer screen, momentarily eclipsing my interviewee as she tells me about the murder that rocked her hometown in New Jersey on 1 May, 1989. 'Sorry, don't mind my cats. Hollie gets a little anxious if I don't pay her enough attention,' says Tracie, reaching for her pet. Hollie, Tracie's 'middle fur baby', emits a contented purr and coils into a glossy heap in her lap.

'The murdered woman's name was Mery Suerez Jara Trusewicz,' Tracie continues. 'I remember when I first heard her name that it sounded unusual. She was just thirty years old and was beaten to death with a hammer and a hacksaw. Just hearing that a woman had been killed in our neighbourhood was scary. Sure, we'd hear of the occasional burglary in Pompton Lakes – but a killing? That was unheard of. The murder scene was less than a ten-minute walk from our family home, too.'

Mery's body was found face up, covered in a bloody sheet and partially under a bed, in the Magnolia Avenue basement apartment she shared with her husband, Jon Trusewicz. And Tracie witnessed, first-hand, captured images of that brutal scene in a series of photographs she viewed at home. Her late father, Patrick Boyle, then a detective in the Pompton Lakes Police Department, had just been assigned the Mery Trusewicz homicide investigation. It was his first murder case and he brought the crime scene photographs home to study as he threw himself into solving it. Tracie's father hadn't wanted his daughter to see these gruesome images, of course, but her curiosity got the better of her.

'That's how I found out about the murder,' explains Tracie. 'Dad brought home the case files and I would watch him poring over the paperwork for hours, every night. Dad's job always fascinated me, but I was curious to know the secrets contained in those papers. So, one day, I crept into the lounge and had a snoop.

'I opened the file and began flicking through the papers, which included photographs of the crime scene. I remember being more intrigued than scared. Then my parents walked into the room and caught me red-handed. They were concerned but, equally, they understood my curiosity. So, they sat me down and explained what had happened at the apartment in Magnolia Avenue. Dad said a young woman had been murdered and now he was trying to figure out who killed her. I was shocked, sad even – to think that somebody could kill a young woman – but mostly, I was intrigued. I asked myself, "Who is Mery's killer and why did they kill her?" Among dozens of other thoughts, I wondered, constantly, "*How will Dad solve this homicide?*"' Tracie, then a wide-eyed sixth grader, had caught the sleuthing bug.

Mery's murder made front page news in New Jersey, with Jon Trusewicz quickly targeted as the prime suspect. Details also emerged about Mery, an 'only child' who had left her parents' home in Peru three years previously to follow her 'dreams' in the US. Press reports painted Mery as a 'slender, stunning woman with dark brown eyes, a bronze complexion and a dazzling smile.' Mery had worked as an attorney in Peru. In New Jersey she'd worked as a secretary for an insurance agency, but she'd planned to go to college and eventually practise law in America. Alas, as the headline in the *Herald News* noted on 4 May, 1989, Mery's 'dream ended in murder.'

According to the *Herald News* article, three days before Mery's body was discovered, Trusewicz called her workplace and said she was ill. He then disappeared – and subsequently became Patrick Boyle's number one suspect for her murder. But, if Trusewicz did kill his wife, then *why* did he kill her? On the surface, Trusewicz, who'd previously served in the navy and the New Jersey National Guard, appeared to have no obvious motive for the crime. A week prior to her death, the couple completed paperwork to buy a house in Pompton Lakes and were due to move in soon. Friends of Mery were quoted in the same *Herald News* article. A fellow Peruvian, named only as Gonzales, described how her friend and Jon married 'because of love. She loved her husband and it seemed like they got along pretty good. She always said good things about him.'

Assuming Trusewicz was the last person to see Mery alive, police launched a nationwide alert to find out his whereabouts. 'We have to find him,' said Patrick Boyle at the time.

'Oh, Dad was determined to find Trusewicz,' says Tracie. 'Dad spent every waking hour on that case and drafted in extra help, too. But with Trusewicz still at large, it was a difficult one to crack. Although that breakthrough did eventually happen.'

Detective Boyle, along with Passaic County Prosecutor's Office investigator, Carlos Rodriguez, meticulously gathered enough evidence, including fingerprints from a saw found at the murder scene, to secure an arrest warrant for murder for Trusewicz on 18 May. The following day, Trusewicz turned up at a hospital in San Francisco. He had taken an overdose of unidentified pills, then called an ambulance to the hotel where he was staying. At the hospital Trusewicz confessed to killing his wife and, after medical treatment, was taken into custody.

'It turned out Trusewicz had travelled through a whole bunch of countries in South America before arriving in California. Now it was Dad's job to fly to San Francisco and escort Trusewicz back to New Jersey to face justice. Back then, this was a huge deal for Dad.' Tracie pauses for a moment and smiles. 'He had never flown before. He was terrified, but I remember my mom and I were both so mad. We were jealous. We wanted to go to California too. Of course, Dad faced his fears about flying, flew to San Francisco with Carlos, and brought Trusewicz back to New Jersey.'

In January 1990, Trusewicz, then twenty-nine, was jailed for thirty years after pleading guilty to aggravated manslaughter. The superior court heard how Trusewicz had flown into a rage after rowing with his wife about money. He admitted slugging Mery with a hammer, cutting her neck with a hacksaw blade, and then gagging her before drawing money from a bank and fleeing to South America.

'I believe Trusewicz got parole after twelve-and-a-half years and is back living in New Jersey. I still think a lot about the case today. It was the kind of case that made me realise how evil people can be. At eleven, it blew my mind that a husband could kill his wife. But, you know, after Trusewicz was caught, everything was alright in the world. Catching Mery's killer was a big deal for Dad. Watching him solve the Mery Trusewicz murder case, I felt so proud. I mean he [Trusewicz] could have just fled and they would never have found him.

'I just knew I wanted to follow in Dad's footsteps, somehow. I told him how I'd like to become an FBI profiler someday, and he encouraged me to follow my dream. Sadly, Dad passed away in 2013, but I will always be so proud of him.'

Tracie didn't join the FBI. But her love for true crime, combined with another passion she developed for ancestry, would lead her to adopt a unique method of sleuthing – a form of powerful, independent detective work that's helping law enforcement agencies solve cold cases in the US while also providing answers for grieving families. When Tracie's not working her day job as an office administrator, she spends countless hours at her computer, comparing DNA samples to databases and studying family trees. Hollie and her two siblings, Callie and Sam, are always at Tracie's side, often pawing at her keyboard when she's working. 'The cats like to get involved,' Tracie says with a laugh.

Tracie is an investigative genetic genealogist and team leader for the DNA Doe Project (DDP). Founded in 2017 by crime-mystery novelist Margaret Press and forensic genealogist Dr Colleen Fitzpatrick, the non-profit US-based organisation is making global headlines for its ground-breaking work. The project's network of dedicated volunteers uses forensic genealogy to 'name' unidentified Jane and John Does, working alongside law enforcement agencies. So far, the DNA Doe Project has named over seventy-five Does – from a man identified with only three cells of DNA extracted from fossilised skeletal remains dating back to 1852, to the victims of serial killers.

Tracie got involved with the DDP in April 2018 after researching her own ancestry – and she has never looked back. Her voice oozes enthusiasm as she relays how her fascination with homicide investigations and television crime dramas took her on an unexpected adventure into genetic crime-solving.

'My interest in true crime intensified into my teenage years and beyond. After Mery's murder, I would ask my dad a bunch of questions about the cases he was working on. But, as I said – Mery's murder aside – not much happened in Pompton Lakes in those days.

'Then, in the nineties, I started watching crime shows. I was – and still am – a huge fan of *The X-Files*. I wanted to be just like *The X-files'* Dana Scully when I grew older. I also love the US crime-procedural comedy-drama, *Bones* – and don't get me started on true crime podcasts. I'm a podcast junkie – and therefore everybody's go-to person when they're looking for a good true crime podcast.

'I've always been an obsessive follower of big murder stories. And the first such case I remember following was the 1994 murders of Nicole Brown Simpson and Ron Goldman, and the subsequent O.J. Simpson trial. I studied the horrific Washington DC sniper attacks closely too, and, more recently, the disappearance and murder of Gabby Petito – who wasn't hooked on that case?

'Around 1998, I started a criminal justice degree at County College of Morris in Randolph, New Jersey. But I ran out of money to fund my studies and, unfortunately, did not get my degree. I wound up in an office job but my curiosity for big crime cases never faltered. And I've always been interested in family history. So, after Dad passed, I decided to take a DNA test and research our family tree. Dad was three when his father, John, passed away, so I never knew much about Dad's side of the family. I wanted to learn more, and that's how my journey into genealogy research began.'

Tracie also asked other relatives to take a test as she delved into her father's heritage. 'Fortunately, my mum had already taken a DNA test, so I could divide the maternal and paternal sides. Then I asked my uncle, Dad's brother, to test. I wanted some DNA other than my own, from Dad. Siblings can get different portions of DNA, so I wanted more representation from an older generation.'

The results surprised Tracie. 'We had always thought that Dad's side of the family was one hundred per cent Irish. Boyle, of course, is a typical Irish surname – and Dad, bless him, was a big proud Irish man. My great-grandfather, John Boyle, was from County Tyrone. He outlived his son, also called John. My mom knew him too – she said he had the "best Irish brogue."

'My dad's brother's DNA results revealed he was 85 per cent Irish. This wasn't a shock to me as, while researching the family tree, I'd found German and New Jersey-Dutch lines. Other lines showed a tiny bit of Irish, so I was like, "*Huh, this all makes sense.*" But Dad's brothers, sisters and cousins didn't believe the results. "No, no, we're *Irish,*" they insisted, which amused me. Thank God my dad wasn't alive to discover the truth. He thought he was Irish through and through. He died thinking he was one hundred per cent Irish.'

Over the next few years, Tracie honed her research skills, immersing herself into the craft that fast became her obsession. She traced adoptees – and helped them find their birth parents.

'My first [adoptee] was my colleague who was searching for her birth father. She had already traced her birth mum, who'd claimed my friend's father was "full Irish." When I delved into the tree, however, I discovered her father was Italian, not Irish. This man had taken a DNA test, which showed as a parent-child match with my friend. I got the results back at Thanksgiving and was able to give my friend her dad's name for her birthday in mid-December.

'Unfortunately, when my friend traced her father, he refused to believe the result – because he couldn't remember her birth mother's name. This happens from time to time. Helping adoptees find their birth parents can be heart-warming and heartbreaking at once. It's wonderful when a reunion goes well. That's the best part – and I frequently receive positive feedback from those I've helped, saying how they've formed beautiful relationships with their biological families. But you can't force people to accept results if they don't believe them. When a parent wants nothing to do with their child, it's difficult. Mostly, my one hope is that I can help give adoptees a sense of belonging, a past, an idea of where they came from. And that's how I ended up getting involved with the Does.'

Tracie's first case with the DDP was to help identify a man in his forties who was found dead in his bed in a Maine apartment. The victim had rented the property using the alias, Alfred Jake Fuller. On 2 May, 2014, Alfred's landlord discovered his tenant's body. At the time, Alfred's death was ruled 'natural' because he had an enlarged heart. However, further investigation revealed no one under the name 'Alfred Jake Fuller' existed in any database.

In September, 2018, at the request of the Maine Office of the Chief Medical Examiner (MOCME), the DDP began the difficult job of finding the man's true identity. The team knew the victim was aged between forty to forty-six, five foot and ten inches tall and weighed 225 pounds. He had light brown-grey curly hair, a short moustache and a goatee beard. He also had a blue discoloration over his left cheek and a large mole between his shoulder blades.

The victim's blood samples were sent to a DNA lab for whole genome sequencing – a test that reads a person's entire genetic code. This produced a file which was then uploaded to

GEDmatch. Following five weeks' extensive family tree research, Tracie and her team identified the man and his relatives.

'I was brand new and learning the ropes,' says Tracie. 'It was a weird case because they thought his name was Alfred Jake Fuller but didn't know if that was his real name. So, we had to do all the matching, find all the common ancestors, and work it through. We pieced it all together eventually. Turned out it was a natural death, and Alfred's real name was never disclosed at his family's request.'

One of Tracie's biggest cases to date, she says, came in 2019 when she helped lead an investigation that went on to identify a female victim of American murderer and serial rapist, Wilson Chouest.

The woman was found dead in an almond orchard in Delano, Kern County, California, on 14 July, 1980. She had been raped and stabbed to death. Believed to be of Hispanic origin, the victim had two distinctive tattoos – a red heart inscribed with 'Shirley. Love you' and a rose surrounded with the words 'Mother' and 'I love you'. Despite media campaigns to identify her, no relatives or friends had come forward. For forty years she remained unidentified, known only as Kern County Jane Doe.

Then, in 2012, DNA extracted from scrapings beneath her fingernails matched with a sample collected from Chouest. The seventy-year-old was serving a life sentence for a string of abductions and rapes when his DNA linked him to Kern County Jane Doe's murder and that of another woman known as Ventura County Jane Doe who had been found dead in a car park in Westlake, Ventura County, California, on 18 July, 1980. Chouest had raped Ventura County Jane Doe and stabbed her sixteen times. He was found guilty of both murders in May 2018. The killer claimed he didn't know either of his two victims and they remained unidentified when he was sentenced.

A DNA sample taken from Kern County Jane Doe's blouse offered just enough decomposed genetic material to prove she was of indigenous descent. 'This was a challenging case,' explains Tracie. 'With these cases we're relying on relatives who've uploaded their DNA to sites such as GEDmatch. Initially we had thought Kern County Jane Doe was of Hispanic origin, and there aren't many Hispanics on GEDmatch. With indigenous cases there's rarely any records, but there are a lot of stories, so you need to look through all the history books and use other people's family trees. In this case, the team searched reams of newspaper articles, looking for reports of missing indigenous women. We need to use information that is out there and hope that it is correct – because, with indigenous cases, it is mostly oral tradition rather than written historical records.'

Kern County Jane Doe's DNA initially returned zero matches on GEDmatch. The team then spent over two thousand hours building hundreds of family trees until, finally, they got a hit. A new upload on GEDmatch turned out to be a half second-cousin of the Doe, meaning the pair shared one great-grandparent. The match also suggested the murdered woman could have recent indigenous ancestry from the Samson Cree Nation from Maskwacis in Alberta, Canada.

The DDP launched an appeal on social media, complete with a reconstruction of Kern County Jane Doe digitally painted by volunteer Carl Koppelman. A response came sooner than expected; just ten days after the appeal went out, the DDP received a call from Violet Soosay, in Alberta, Canada. Violet had seen Carl's rendering on Facebook and thought the woman in the picture resembled her missing aunt, Shirley Ann Soosay, who vanished without trace in 1979. Violet had been looking for Shirley – who was in her thirties when she went missing – ever since. She'd searched graveyards, hospitals, parks and bars all over Canada. She'd even travelled to Seattle to hunt for her missing relative after hearing that Shirley may have visited a friend there.

'Violet had been searching for her aunty for four decades,' says Tracie. 'The last time she'd seen Shirley was at a funeral in 1977. Violet had made a promise to Shirley's mother [Violet's grandmother] that she would never give up looking for her daughter. Shirley's mother died in 1991 but Violet continued to search for her aunt. When Violet saw Carl's picture and the ancestry information we put out, she believed there was a strong possibility that Kern County Jane Doe could be her aunty. Violet uploaded her DNA to GEDmatch and we got to work.'

Violet's inkling was correct. By April 2021, the DDP announced the identification of Kern County Jane Doe as thirty-five-year-old Shirley Ann Soosay. She was one of the first indigenous Does to be named using genetic genealogy. Shirley's remains, previously buried in a California graveyard under the name 'Kern County Jane Doe', were returned to her family in Alberta. On the day of Shirley's funeral, Violet spoke of her relief that her aunt had 'come home'. She told the Aboriginal People's Television Network (APTN): 'Most of all today, I feel relief that I was able to keep the promise I made to my grandmother – of finding Shirley and bringing her home. This is the final step. It's no more not knowing. No more uncertainty. We are certain that she's home now and certain that we can visit her gravesite.'

When I ask Tracie how it felt to solve a forty-year mystery, she shakes her head a little. 'Oh, I can't take credit for solving this case. I did some research at the beginning, but mainly I was co-leading. Another volunteer made the Cree ancestry connection – and, of course, Carl's amazing picture was pivotal. But, yes, we felt good, as a team, to have been able to help return Shirley to her family.'

As if on cue, Hollie stirs and jumps onto the desk again. Tracie laughs as the cat mooches off camera. Her pet's sudden movement reminds her of the first time she solved a Doe case single-handed. 'It was a moment – that moment – when Hollie high-fived me,' she says. 'I was excited about my first solve. Hollie was on the desk. I pushed my palm towards her and said, "High five, Hollie," and she lifted her little paw and tapped my hand. It was probably a coincidence but, hey, I like to think that she meant it.'

'I think she meant it,' I assure her.

Tracie was looking at obituaries when she made her breakthrough in the 2004 case of Phoenix Jane Doe – a woman, aged between thirty-five and fifty, found rolled in a carpet and dumped by a roadside in Glendale, Phoenix. Her corpse had decayed to bones encased in a sports bra, a T-shirt, a blue zip-up jacket, and a checked flannel shirt. A pair of non-prescription glasses, a black plastic watch and a diamond earring were found with her body. The investigation had lain cold for fifteen years when Phoenix Police Department's Detective Stuart Somershoe submitted a DNA sample taken from the Doe's skeletal remains to the DDP.

While building family trees based on small percentage matches on the database, Tracie found an obituary for a woman named Elizabeth Ann Bibb, who had died in 2016, aged seventy-nine. The obituary mentioned that she was survived by a daughter, Ginger Lynn Bibb, from Glendale. Tracie couldn't find any further information on Elizabeth, but Ginger Bibb's birth certificate looked promising. Ginger was born in May 1958, which placed her in the right age bracket as Phoenix Jane Doe. And the Doe's body was discovered in Glendale, which tallied with the information on Elizabeth's death certificate.

'We were working on the ancestry lines – starting with grandparents or great grandparents and building down to the children's level – and that's how I found Elizabeth's obituary naming her daughter. It all seemed to add up to me, so I went with my spider sense.'

Tracie called the tip in to her team leader, her voice tinged with just enough insouciance. 'Best not to sound too overconfident at this stage,' she explains. 'You always want to go into these things with an open mind. It's difficult – we all go with our spider senses sometimes, but you don't want to have confirmation bias.

'My team leader, Karen, agreed Ginger Lynn Bibb could be a possible match. So, we started investigating further, along with more volunteers. We were looking for proof of life for Ginger Lynn Bibb but nobody could find anything about her post 2004. There was no death certificate for her, either. Phoenix Jane Doe's DNA matches weren't close so, at this point, we needed to make sure we had links to both sides of the family tree before we submitted Ginger Lynn Bibb as a potential candidate to the detectives. Which we did do – less than two days after I found her name in the [her mother's] obituary.'

As Tracie points out, the next stage took time; once the DDP has presented its findings to detectives, they must then conduct their own investigations before approaching family members. 'They [the police] also need to check for proof of life for that person. They'll gather as much information on the Doe as they can – look for dental records if they're available. Only once everything looks good will they talk to the potential candidate's relatives and ask them for DNA samples.'

Detectives, also, found no proof of life for Ginger Lynn Bibb past 2004. They could find no missing person report filed for her either. Confident with the DDP's prediction, they approached Ginger's father, who agreed to submit a DNA sample.

'It was a match,' says Tracie, beaming. 'Phoenix Jane Doe now has a name – and that name is Ginger Lynn Bibb.'

9

Don't F**k with Cats

Spätkauf café, Berlin, 4 June, 2012, 11.54 a.m.

'There's something familiar about him,' *thinks Kadir Anlayisli, squinting at the figure in sunglasses through the window of the internet café. The guy he is watching strides purposefully along Karl-Marx-Strasse, cutting a sharp outline in the June sunshine. His posture is straight yet relaxed, left arm swinging in time with his step – he has a confident gait. The man turns and glides through the open café door, props his shades atop his head, and approaches café worker Kadir at the counter. 'Bonjour, sir. Internet?' he says, hands mining deep into the front pockets of his jeans. The deep, slow drawl belies its owner's youthful face.*

The man is in his late twenties, Kadir guesses. He's polite, with model-like features: a slightly upturned nose, curvy lips and sharp, manicured brows. 'Weird cheekbones though, which also look familiar.' *His hair is fawn and razored – a three-blade cut – and he's wearing make-up. Kadir smiles and makes his way round the counter. He gestures left, up a few steps and into the tight throat of the café which houses the boxy computer terminals.* 'Follow me,' *he says.* 'There are thirty-six internet booths. I will show you.' *Kadir assigns booth number twenty-five, and the man sits down.*

Over an hour passes. Net surfers come and go but the occupant of cubicle twenty-five remains and, for some reason, Kadir can't stop thinking about him. A twister of questions whizzes around in his head. 'That face . . . it's so distinct. Has he been here before? I've seen him somewhere.' *Then, morbid recognition sinks in, flashbacks of news articles Kadir read just this morning. Panic roils in his chest, prickles his neck and sours his mouth.* 'Is that really him? If so, why would he risk coming in here? What shall I do? What is he looking at online?'

Heart rattling, Kadir wanders up to the computer booths, where he grabs a nearby rubbish bin and an ashtray and pretends to clean up. But his gaze is fixed on the man ensconced in booth twenty-five. He freezes for a moment, throwing a sideways glance towards the bright text scrolling up the screen. The man in the booth pushes his face closer to the monitor, attention seemingly piqued at the Interpol alert that shouts in gore red about the international manhunt for Luka Rocco Magnotta – a suspected cannibal killer on the run from Montreal, Canada.

With a plasticky scratch and two clicks of the mouse, the reader summons a fresh page. A news article appears showing a picture of the Canadian fugitive beneath the headline: 'Cops Hunt Porn Star For Snuff Vid Killing.' A sub-heading reads, 'Horror as body parts are sent in the mail.' Click, click, another report bearing the same picture and the words, 'Canadian Psycho has been spotted in Paris.' The news rolls on. 'Body parts fugitive Luka Rocco Magnotta added to Interpol's wanted list.' Kadir drops the ashtray contents into the bin and takes a couple of shaky steps backwards as he suddenly realises: the man in booth number twenty-five is Luka Rocco Magnotta.

Kadir puts down the bin and quietly edges away from booth twenty-five, careful not to disturb its occupant. The seriousness of the situation is overwhelming. A suspected murderer – a cannibal – and Canada's most wanted fugitive, is here in this café, googling himself among innocent customers. Other users will be reading the news, Kadir suspects, and they too might recognise Magnotta. 'Gently does it. Stay cool. If Magnotta knows I'm on to him, he could turn violent, pull out a knife – an ice pick even? Most likely, he'll flee.'

He heads down the five steps, then Kadir quickens his pace to the front door, surreptitiously glancing, once – and then twice – over his shoulder. He shuttles through the doorway, into the blazing sunshine where, miraculously, he sees a police van approaching. He runs into the road, towards the vehicle, arms violently slashing the air. The van pulls over and Inspector Marc Lilge jumps out, followed by eight camouflaged trainee cadets. Kadir's face shines but his voice is measured when he gestures with a twitch of his head at the café's open door behind him. 'There's somebody in there that I'm sure you're looking for,' he tells the inspector, then he turns and, arms folded across his chest, calmly leads Inspector Lilge and his team inside the café.

They head up the steps to booth twenty-five, where Magnotta is still basking in news that he is a wanted man – until he feels a tap on his right shoulder, hears his name spoken. In German-accented English: 'Luka Magnotta? Can I see some identification, please?'

Magnotta twists in his seat, looks up at Lilge with confusion while his picture stares back at him with penicillium-blue eyes from the computer screen. 'I'm Kirk Trammell,' he says with a nervous smile. 'I'm from New York. I'm in town visiting friends.' Encircled by cadets, there's nowhere for Magnotta to run. Other café clients emerge from their cubicles, keen to see what all the fuss is about.

'Let's go over there and talk,' offers Lilge, nodding into the right hand corner of the room. Magnotta rises shakily but accompanies the officer as the cadets form a wall at the top of the steps. Once in the corner, Lilge again asks Magnotta for identification – and notices how the fugitive's face is slick with sweat. His hands are trembling too and, when Magnotta finally replies, his pitch is high and arrhythmic.

'You got me,' he says. 'I'm Mr Magnotta, I'm the man you're looking for.'

Magnotta does not resist or complain when handcuffed, his only concern being that they leave the café quickly – 'before the media arrives.' Throughout the journey to the police station, Magnotta sits calmly in the van, grinning.

He looks almost relieved. Or is he reliving his heinous crimes in his head? Either way, Luka Rocco Magnotta has been arrested, ironically captured on account of his insatiable narcissism. A jury will later convict him of first-degree murder, and he'll serve life behind bars.

Six days before the killer walked into Kadir's internet café, the headless torso of Magnotta's lover, Jun Lin, was found stuffed inside a battered suitcase in an alley outside Magnotta's home – a low-rent 1960s apartment block at 5720 Decarie Boulevard, in Montreal's Snowdon district. Janitor Mike Nadeau spotted the suitcase dumped among rubbish bags and wondered why the luggage was locked. Suspicious, he prised open the suitcase and recoiled with shock at what he found inside. The case was alive with thousands of maggots, and the smell was suffocatingly putrid. Nadeau immediately reported his gruesome find to Montreal Police, who launched a murder investigation.

Within three days, detectives identified the victim as thirty-three-year-old Chinese engineering student Jun Lin, who'd been reported missing by friends the same day that Nadeau discovered his decaying torso. CCTV surveillance cameras captured Jun entering the property with Magnotta on the evening of 24 May, 2012. Devastatingly, Jun had no idea he was walking to his death, or that his killer would film his horrific murder inside apartment 208 and post the chilling footage on a gore site just hours after the slaying. The video, titled *1 Lunatic 1 Ice Pick* went viral – then Luka Magnotta fled the country.

As the international manhunt for Magnotta swung into action, more shocking evidence of Jun's murder emerged in scenes reminiscent of a slasher film. Packaged body parts, later confirmed as Jun's, arrived in the post at two Vancouver primary schools. Then Jun's left foot turned up at Conservative Party of Canada's headquarters in Ottawa. His left hand was also seized at a post office, in a package addressed to the Liberal Party. The remains were wrapped in pink tissue paper and accompanied by menacing notes and poems. In one note, scrawled on pink paper with a blue marker pen, the murderer warns: 'Roses are red, violets are blue, the police will need dental records to identify you, bitch.'

Meanwhile, police announced that Magnotta had left Montreal on an Air Transat flight to Paris. Footage showed Magnotta ambling through a security checkpoint at Charles De Gaulle Airport. In that clip, Magnotta is wearing a chin-length dark wig and a T-shirt picturing a vintage Mickey Mouse. The hunt for Magnotta then centred around Paris, where police believed him to still be – until the morning Kadir recognised him.

Without Kadir's quick-thinking actions, Luka Rocco Magnotta – real name Eric Newman – might still be at large today. Crime experts say Magnotta most definitely would have killed again had he not been apprehended. But it's also thanks to a global army of animal-loving internet sleuths that Magnotta was finally unmasked and caught. And it all started with a disturbing video featuring cats.

The short film, *1 boy 2 kittens* debuted on YouTube on 21 December, 2010. Posted by a user named uonlywish500, the video's opening scene suggests a display of fluffy cuteness will follow. In a small bedroom, two tabby kittens lay side by side on a silver bedspread decorated with an image of a lone wolf. John Lennon's 'Happy Xmas (War is Over)' plays in the background as the camera zooms in on the animals. A human hand creeps into shot and strokes the kittens. Then the footage jumps to a longer shot showing the kittens, still curled up on the wolf bedcover – alongside a vacuum storage bag. A male figure in a teal hoodie walks into the frame, leans over the bed, and scoops up the kittens. As he turns, we catch a fleeting glimpse of his profile. He has a pert nose, an unlit cigarette is clamped between his lips, and a flop of muddy fringe falls from the hem of his hood, obscuring his eyes. There's a sticky rustle of plastic as he feeds the kittens into the vacuum bag, and the scene that follows sends the internet into a frenzy of outrage and disgust.

The young man attaches a hose to the bag and suddenly John Lennon is drowned by the hollow vrooms of a vacuum cleaner. The bag shrinks around the defenceless animals, suffocating them in less than a few seconds. One kitten tries, unsuccessfully, to escape from the bag.

Appalled by this atrocious act, animal activists launched an online crusade to identify the mystery kitten killer who, according to them, had violated the internet's ultimate rule: Don't fuck with cats. A Facebook group called 'Find the Vacuum Killer for Great Justice' was set up and thousands of sickened internet users from all corners of the world joined the group's campaign to find the identity of the cat torturer – before he killed again.

The sleuths' eighteen-month quest was the subject of the 2019 Netflix docuseries, *Don't F**k with Cats: Hunting an Internet Killer*. Set over three hour-long episodes, the series features two of the group's stalwart members – Deanna Thompson, from Las Vegas, and a Los Angeles resident known by his alias 'John Green'.

Don't F**k with Cats makes for unsettling yet gripping viewing. In the opening scene we meet Deanna, a data analyst by day, who speaks from her lamp-lit Vegas living room. As she speaks, demonic string music partners her words. A montage of flash stills of the internet follies she describes crosses the screen – comedy videos of people falling over, emojis, share buttons, the demolition of a building.

'The internet is boundless, right?' says Deanna. 'I mean it's the Wild West. There are the happy places where you look at cute-looking babies, pictures of your kids going to school. But, more than anything, people love looking at cats.

'Then there's another part of the internet that's a free for all. The seedy underbelly. Porn, violence, somebody getting pushed down the stairs. Street fights, bum fights, defamatory pictures of the Statue of Liberty. And nobody gives a crap. Nobody's going to bat an eye. But in this seedy underbelly there's an unwritten rule. Now, it's unwritten but it's understood . . .' The music crescendos and quickens to an agitated pace. '. . . It's rule zero. And rule zero is . . .' Deanna jabs her index finger in the air four times as the camera closes in on her face. 'Don't. Fuck. With. Cats.'

Deanna, whose online alter ego, Baudi Moovan, is inspired by the Beastie Boys track 'Body Moovin', first encountered *1 boy 2 kittens* when a link to the video appeared on her Facebook feed. Being a cat-lover and, in her words, a 'textbook definition of a computer nerd', she couldn't resist clicking on the YouTube link. Like many others, she expected a parade of kitty loveliness to ooze through her laptop screen – which was just the tonic she needed in December 2010, as her relationship had just come to 'a pretty drastic end.'

'I was really fucked up about it [the relationship ending] in the head. I just wanted to sink my mind into . . . kind of . . . not deal with this bullshit in my life. And so, I was on Facebook one day and I found a post. A lot of people had been feverishly posting about a video that was online. I thought, "*Let's go look at this.*"' Deanna pressed play and her heart swelled when she saw the two huddled kittens. 'I'm thinking, "*Oh, cute video! Look at this.*"' But when the footage turned sinister, Deanna had to switch it off. She could not bear to watch the inevitable fate of those innocent felines.

For the documentary though, she views and narrates the entire video on her purple laptop for the camera. Her voice cracks when she reaches brutal ending. 'He's attaching a vacuum hose to the area of the bag where the vacuum hose would seal into. One of the kittens playfully tries to get out of the bag and, y'know . . .' Deanna chokes. '. . . It's fucking heartbreaking, dude.' The vacuum whirrs and Deanna pauses to wipe her flooding eyes. 'I fucking hate this shit. It's so sad. I love cats. I *love* them. And there are prices to pay. Consequences for this.'

While Deanna was admittedly horrified by the video, she says some comments it attracted also shocked her. 'I wasn't the only one who was outraged. The comments below this video were like, "I can't believe this motherfucker's doing this." And, "Who the fuck is this guy? Let's kill him." It was like, outrage, just – boom, boom, boom, boom. And I get it, this is an emotional thing. But who the hell are you gonna call? Which police department are you gonna call because you don't know where this happened? This person could live in, you know, Siberia for all I know.' It was amid the torrent of vitriol, that Deanna found the link to 'Find the Vacuum Killer for Great Justice'. Deanna joined. This group seemed focussed in its pursuit to unveil the identity of the man behind the evil video. One member caught Deanna's attention for his 'non-emotional' ability to 'stick to the facts.' That person went by the name of John Green.

In the Netflix series, John says his obsession with hunting the kitten killer heightened when he viewed the culprit's profile. There, he noticed uonlywish500 had 'liked' a trailer to Steven Spielberg's 2002 movie, *Catch Me If You Can*, in which Leonardo DiCaprio plays a conman Frank Abagnale. That told John something about the individual behind the profile.

'What kind of individual thinks, I'm going to take a vacuum sealed bag and place two kittens in it?' says John in the documentary. 'When I clicked on the user's profile, I noticed they had a video for the film *Catch Me If You Can*. I took that as, "Hey, you're never going to find me. Ha-ha, fuck you." I thought, "*This person wants to play a game of cat and mouse – and I'm up for that.*"

Deanna contacted John with some ideas on how to identify the man in the video. 'The Facebook group was trying to find out who the culprit was. I thought this was weird. You can't find a person, but you *can* find objects in a room that would tell you *where* this person is,' she says.

And so, Deanna and John, along with other members, began a forensic investigation of the *1 boy 2 kittens* video. John created a 'schematical diagram' of the bedroom in the video based on the footage. He estimated the room measured ten by eight feet. His computerised aerial drawing depicted a bed in the centre of the room, its head touching the left width wall. Abutting the bed's right side, a chair sat in front of the bedroom door. A fridge stood against the right length wall, while a television and a figurine crowned a table to the left of the bed. The drawing also indicated a wastepaper basket bin against the wall facing the foot of the bed.

The sleuths studied objects in the room – light fittings, plug sockets, the door handle and the furniture. The lone wolf bedspread was a prominent feature. 'This wolf blanket was hideous and super unique,' Deanna recalls in the series. She found the blanket for sale on eBay and discovered the bedding was made by a company in North America and that they had sold just one blanket. Alas, they were not able to give her access the buyer's details and the blanket was shipped internationally, which meant its owner could be 'anywhere on the planet.' Another hunt for the bedroom door handle saw Deanna investing 'sixteen hours looking at doorknobs from Lithuania.'

Scrutinising the video's audio highlighted a clue that would direct the group to Russia. John and Deanna detected another voice filtering through the lyrics of 'Happy Xmas (War is

Over)'. Did this mean there was a second person in the room when the kittens were suffocated? It sounded like an Eastern Bloc accent, they decided. A Ukrainian sleuther who went by the alias Nicee Punk recognised the accent as Russian and, after weeks of further investigating, the group traced the voice. It belonged to an actor in a Russian soap opera. The team even matched the dialogue to a specific episode. Had the man in the video inserted a second recording into the mix to throw anyone trying to identify him off the scent? 'At this point I thought, "*This person is playing games, trying to mislead us,*"' says John.

Despite their dogged efforts – long hours and sleepless nights spent trawling the web – all these potential leads resulted in dead ends for the citizen investigators. And then, there was another morbid twist in the puzzle.

In early 2011, the cat killer returned to the internet with a second video. In this instalment, viewers are reunited with the teal-hooded man, back in the bedroom where he killed the cats. The camera zooms on the lone wolf blanket, then sways up to reveal a patch of urine-coloured wall before falling and twisting left. Now we see the figure in the hood – and he's playing with the kittens he killed, arranging their stiff bodies on the wolf blanket to the soundtrack of John Lennon's 'Imagine'.

What was even more disturbing was that a link to the video appeared on the group's Facebook page. The kitten murderer had infiltrated the Facebook group. The link was posted by John Smith – an account the group instantly knew was a fake account, or a 'sock puppet account' as Deanna describes it. 'A sock puppet account is usually very easy to recognise. It has a super-generic name, with a super generic profile picture. They will post something, then delete the account.'

Deanna clicked on the link and shuddered: a face-on shot of the cat killer, lounging on his bed while holding the two dead kittens. He'd blurred his face in the image but he'd posted it deliberately in the Facebook group of people who were working to identify him. 'This was so important,' says Deanna, 'because it gave us an insight into who this guy was. Maybe he wants to be chased a little bit? It's almost like he was saying, "Are you guys stupid? I'm gonna throw you this bone and see how you gnaw on it for a little while." But the second thing this told us he was that he was following the investigation. And what other accounts was he using?'

After the second video was posted, some members of the Justice group began to worry about their personal safety. But despite their fears, the sleuthers forged on. For most, the cat killer's infiltration into their group fuelled their determination to find him.

One member of the group, who uses the alias Maia S. Abdulhalim Amina Guerrero, shared her recollections of that time with me in a series of text messages. Due to serious health issues, Maia could not speak with me in person. She tells me that the collective nightmare the group's members shared was that the animal slayer would 'kill a human next.' 'I was just a member of our group. It was a team effort,' Maia insists. 'We were all equals with different talents, knowledge and abilities that we shared to accomplish our common goal.'

Maia, now seventy-five, studied law enforcement at college in the eighties. She says, 'The one thing that initially brought the group together was our deep love of animals and our mission to seek justice against all animal abusers – and this is what led us to track down the cat killer. It was terrifying to know that, while we were tracking him, he was stalking us too. And taunting us – as were an assortment of his sicko admirers. Many of us used pseudonyms to safeguard ourselves and our families. But we knew we had to find the cat killer and get him off the streets before he killed again. We were all so sure he would escalate to killing a human before too long.'

In the wake of John Smith's posting of the second video, the Facebook set ramped up their efforts. One useful factor about the second video was that they now had more objects on show in the room. John Green downloaded every frame from the videos – 'tens of thousands of them' – as single images to ensure no stone was left unturned. Repeated viewings of the videos and the still frames from the film would engender new discoveries.

'We were fired-up,' says Deanna. 'In the videos, everything moves so fast, but now we had individual images on which to focus.' In one frame, Deanna spotted a packet of cigarettes nesting in the wolf blanket. By enlarging the image, she could see the government health warning on the side of the Marlboro Lights pack from the 'Surgeon General'. At last, a breakthrough. This meant the cigarettes were bought in North America. 'This was a huge piece of evidence. Now, this person could have bought a pack of cigarettes and then hopped on a plane to Paris or Berlin. But I knew they were North American cigarettes.'

Buoyed by her discovery, Deanna continued trawling the stills until she stumbled upon another piece of useful evidence: a clear shot of the murder weapon. A yellow vacuum cleaner was parked on the salmon carpet next to the rubbish bin. Deanna posted the image on a vacuum repair forum online along with the message, 'Anyone know this vacuum?' Seconds later, somebody replied, naming the model as a Kenmore 721.26082 – a vacuum cleaner only sold in North America. 'So, we now know that – whomever this guy is who made the video – we can start looking [for him] in Mexico, the United States or Canada.'

But just as the sleuthers thought they were making progress on the case, a hardcore animal rights group, Rescue Ink, intervened, offering a $5,000 reward for information leading to the cat killer's identity. Rescue Ink is a team of tattooed motorcyclists based in Long Island, New York who work together to combat animal cruelty. Joe 'Panz' Panzarella, a leader of Rescue Ink, describes the organisation's work as an 'in-your-face approach to animal abuse and neglect.' 'We do whatever is necessary within the realms of the law to rescue animals out of bad situations,' he says in the Netflix documentary.

While pleased that the reward attracted attention to the cause, the Justice group suddenly found themselves deluged with a tidal wave of new members bringing with them some less than useful posts. CGI 'experts' posted their impressions of the culprit's face. Vigilantes posted profiles of innocent people with similar features to the guy in *1 boy 2 kittens*, with messages reading, 'It might be him!' Admins for the Justice group deleted the posts as swiftly as they appeared, but they could not control the thousands of messages swamping Rescue Ink's Facebook page.

Then, on 8 January, 2011, a member called Jamsey Cramsalot Inhisass posted on Rescue Ink's reward site: 'I step on little kittens and make videos of it.' His profile picture showed a side-on shot of a man in his twenties. He had chin-length ochre hair with a floppy fringe falling from under the brim of a Santa hat. Not only did he resemble the kitten executioner – he'd posted a video of a kitten burning to death in a cage. Convinced Jamsey 'very well could be the guy,' Panzarella enlisted a female group member to message the profile. A Facebook dialogue ensued between the pair, and, after a few exchanges, the woman asked Jamsey, 'Are you the guy who did *1 boy 2 kittens?*'

Jamsey speedily replied, 'Yes I kill kittens LOL.'

The exchange was revealed to the rest of the group. A celebratory video of blasting fireworks appeared on Rescue Ink's page. Inflamed responses followed. 'I hope someone finds him and does the same to him as he did to those kittens. Bastard,' wrote one member. Rescue Ink was convinced Jamsey was the man behind the video. But the Justice group wanted more evidence. So, they returned to Jamsey's profile picture, and uploaded it to TinEye Reverse Image – a search engine for tracing the origin of pictures. Their search led them to a gay porn site, 19 nitten. On the homepage they boasted: '19 nitten is one of the oldest Gay sites featuring only original photos of the cutest 18+ gay teen boys. All photos are shot by our own dedicated team of photographers and are exclusive to this site.'

'So, we're scrolling through all these pictures,' says Deanna. 'You know, next, next, next, and then . . . boom.' In the gallery of young men, they struck gold: Sandwiched between 'Markus' and 'Joel' was Jamsey's profile picture, minus the Santa hat. His porn name was Timmy. Of course, Jamsey had not used his own image for the profile.

'So, we knew Jamsey had appropriated that picture and added a photoshopped Santa hat,' Deanna explains. Despite warnings from the Justice group that the man in the profile picture was probably not the cat killer, the Rescue Ink Facebook group pursued him. They flooded Jamsey's page with threats. 'Listen you sick fuck, you better watch your back,' wrote one user. The reign of intimidation continued:

'We know who you are.'

'We know where you are.'

'Be scared, little boy.'

'We're coming for you.'

Justice members traced Jamsey to a town in South Africa. It turned out he was not the kitten slayer, but an internet troll named Eduard Louis Jordaan. Soon after the online attacks from members of Rescue Ink's Facebook group, Eduard died by suicide. 'Months later we found out Eduard had been dealing with depression,' says Deanna. 'He'd spent a lot of time online, avoiding that depression. Nobody knows – and I'm certainly not saying – that he killed himself because of this witch hunt against him. But you do have to be careful because you don't know who's on the other end of the computer and what kind of mental problems they might have.'

Amid all the false accusations against Jamsey, Justice group member, Nicee Punk's inbox bleeped. The message came from another sock puppet account holder named Beverly Kent. 'The person you're looking for . . . his name is Luka Magnotta,' she declared.

Beverly's revelation both baffled and intrigued the group. After the Jamsey debacle, members were understandably sceptical. Could this be another troll spouting fake information? The intrepid sleuths had only one way to find out.

Fingers sprinted over keyboards, repeatedly tapping 'Luka Magnotta' into Google. Hundreds of search results for 'Luka Magnotta' beamed on computer screens. The results were astonishing – unbelievable almost. Magnotta was ubiquitous on the internet. YouTube featured a Luka Magnotta picture slideshow set to New Order's 'True Faith'. The montage, which is still online today, exhibits a young man with a sculpted face and glossed lips. That tilted nose and floppy fringe are unmistakeable. In a succession of photographs, Magnotta postures in an array of outfits. He pouts moodily in a red, sleeveless hoodie, reclines on a sunbed in miniscule trunks. In many shots, Magnotta is bare chested. He tries to emulate James Dean, popping the collar of his biker jacket in the style of the late Hollywood actor.

Further searches pulled user-generated fan sites loaded with more photographs of Magnotta living, what appeared to be, a champagne, jet-setting lifestyle. There were photos of Magnotta on a beach in Bermuda, cradling a baby spider monkey and squinting at the sun and Magnotta in Russia's Red Square. The Trevi Fountain in Rome provided the backdrop to another portrait of Magnotta in a black cap and shades. He appeared in New York's Times Square and in front of the Eiffel Tower in Paris. There was Magnotta in a limo, in a hot tub and lounging on a zebra-print rug. Fans had left fawning comments, labelling Magnotta 'hot', 'beautiful', 'sexy' and 'handsome'.

Rumours abounded on the message boards of these sites – outlandish stories claimed Magnotta was a model and a 'long-lost cousin' of deceased actor River Phoenix. 'Luka Magnotta is dating Madonna,' it was alleged. None of this added up. Nobody had heard of Luka Magnotta until now.

However, there was a definite familiarity about his appearance. His bone structure and hair certainly mirrored that of the kitten killer. In *Don't F**k with Cats*, Deanna recalls how she was wary of 'ringing alarm bells.' 'Given the group's history of accusing the wrong people, I was very hesitant to start talking to the group about who this person was yet.' Erring on the side of caution, she and John set up a new, private Facebook group, *Luka_Intel*, and invited a selection of trusted Justice group members to join.

They had a name now but, without knowing Magnotta's location, it was back to the drawing board for the internet detectives. The internet threw up a new clue. Magnotta had auditioned for a reality television show on the Canadian LGBT channel OUTtv – and footage of his pitch was on YouTube. The 2007 programme, *Cover Guy*, aimed to find the ultimate male underwear model. Magnotta fancied his chances and, in the video, he appears before the judging panel sporting a boyband-style, cropped peroxide hairdo. He speaks with a North American accent. Finally, the investigators could put a voice to Magnotta's face.

In the clip, Magnotta exudes arrogance and confidence. After asking Magnotta to remove his shirt, a judge remarks on his 'low voice'. Magnotta slowly sheds his shirt and replies, 'I have a very deep voice. A lot of people tell me that, actually.'

A second judge asks, 'So, how do you get your voice so deep?' Magnotta slings his shirt over one shoulder and gestures at his throat. 'How do I get my voice so deep? Practice makes perfect, right?' He illustrates this comment with an egomaniacal smirk and a poke of his tongue. 'A lot of people tell me I'm really devastatingly good-looking,' he goes on. The judges are impressed but say they want to see a beefier physique. 'We're going to ask you to come back on the show next year,' they say. 'It's a tiebreaker.' Magnotta's smile shines as bright as the gold chain wreathing his neck.

At the time, Deanna wondered, 'Can this person really be somebody who films himself putting cats into a vacuum bag and sucking all the air out until they suffocate? As I'm watching, I'm thinking, "No, *this can't be the same guy.*" And then I got a message from John Green.' Poring over Magnotta's snaps from around the world, John noticed considerable inconsistencies in the images.

'Looking at all these Luka photographs you start seeing a pattern,' he says. 'I thought, "*Wait a minute, that face doesn't appear to match that body.*" You'd start noticing lines. Things had been edited or didn't line up correctly.' Magnotta had superimposed his head onto the bodies of random people he'd found on the internet. Furthermore, when the sleuths re-examined Magnotta's fan sites – around forty of them – it became clear that they too must have been fabricated by him. The so-called fans' gushing comments read the same on all pages.

More rumours appeared on forums – including one that was followed up by journalist Joe Warmington at the *Toronto Sun* newspaper in 2007. Driving home from work one evening, Joe heard Magnotta's 'frantic' voice on a popular radio show. Magnotta had called the station to deny claims he'd dated Canadian serial killer Karla Homolka. Homolka had acted as an accomplice to her husband, Paul Bernardo, who raped and murdered three teenage girls, including Homolka's younger sister, Tammy. The media had dubbed the couple the Barbie and Ken killers – due to their good looks and wealthy background.

'He [Magnotta] was upset about how he'd been labelled with being romantically involved with Karla Homolka,' Joe told me. 'I had covered the Homolka and Bernardo case. Homolka is known as the most evil woman in Canada. Luckily, the caller said his name on air – Luka Magnotta – so I wrote it down. When I got home, I googled his name and saw that he had an incredible online presence. I tracked Magnotta down, reached out to him via email, and out of nowhere, he called me. He wanted me to go to meet him somewhere – I can't remember where – but I didn't feel comfortable with that, so I invited him into the *Sun* newsroom, which he agreed to. Knowing what I know now, that was the right decision to meet him at the office.

'When Luka Magnotta walked into the newsroom, I couldn't believe my eyes. This guy looked just like Paul Bernardo. He had similar short, bleached blond hair to Bernardo.'

Fortunately for the sleuths, Joe filmed his 2007 interview with Magnotta and the footage was included in the online version of the story, headlined 'Homolka rumour ruins model's life'. During the interview, Magnotta told Joe how his modelling career had 'gone downhill' in the wake of the Homolka claims. He said he wanted to 'set the record straight' and stressed, 'Me and her have absolutely no connection.' Magnotta claimed his life was spiralling out of control. 'I'm getting death threats,' he says in the interview. 'I'm having a nervous breakdown. My reputation is completely ruined.'

'I was pretty worried about him,' recalls Joe. 'I thought maybe he had mental health issues – and, at the time, I wrote the column more along the lines of trying to give this guy some help.'

After watching the interview, Deanna suspected the Homolka story to be another figment of Magnotta's warped imagination. Had Magnotta spread the rumour himself to gain notoriety? 'Like, why would you want to associate with a serial killer?' she asks. 'For fame? A 100 per cent. It really made me think his motivation . . . was the attention and the fame that he *knew* he would get from it. And he got it.' As the group gleaned more insight into Magnotta's psyche, the more they believed him to be the cat killer.

Despite Magnotta's egotistical presence on the worldwide web his seventy-plus sock puppet accounts, YouTube slideshows and reality TV show audition – the *Luku_Intel* group still had no idea where he lived. Joe Warmington's interview placed Magnotta in Toronto in 2007, but he could since have moved anywhere in the world. *Luka_Intel* was determined to find him. Working through the night and around their day jobs, the citizen investigators scrutinised Magnotta's photographs, hoping he'd 'left a digital footprint somewhere.' Luckily, he had.

Among the thousands of pouting snaps Magnotta had plastered over the internet was a photo of him standing on a third or fourth floor balcony of an apartment block. In this photo, Magnotta is sporting a short, spiky brown haircut and heavy, accentuated brows that look marker-penned on. He's wearing a white puffer jacket and staring directly into the lens, his expression sulky and his face speckled with falling snowflakes. The picture had not been photoshopped. This time, the sleuths had clues to work with in the snowy vista behind him.

The balcony overlooks an intersection housing a petrol station on one corner. Its red signage carrying Canada's maple leaf symbol told John this was a Petro-Canada garage. Looming behind the petrol station was another apartment block – a grey building of around twenty storeys.

'So, the first thing I do is jump onto Google Maps,' says John. 'And, literally, there are hundreds of Petro-Canada gas stations. But I start cross-refencing things, and I remember, Luka made this blog post, talking about how the paparazzi was harassing him, how they were trying to take his picture outside his condo in Etobicoke, Canada. And I thought, hmm, that's interesting. Etobicoke – where's that?'

Etobicoke, John discovered, is a suburb in west Toronto, home to some 365,000 residents, lush green spaces, and six Petro-Canada gas stations. John returned to Google Maps, clicked on the red flags indicating the stations' locations, then looked them up on Google Street View. John's third click transported him to the corner of an intersection, where a grey cement apartment block towered over a Petro-Canada station.

The excitement in John's voice is palpable as he shares his next move, which he mimes to camera in the docuseries. Gripping an imaginary computer mouse, he slowly swipes his hand left, slicing a smooth, horizontal arc in the air. 'I take my curser, and I rotate the street view a hundred and eighty degrees – and I'm looking directly at the apartment in which Luka is seen in the photograph. So now, I've got this fucker.' The address John was looking at was 304 Mill Road, Etobicoke.

John reported his bombshell discovery to Toronto Police who, after initial resistance, investigated his claims. Officers headed to the Mill Road apartment where Magnotta was pictured, but there was no sign of him there. 'They knocked on the door. A person answered, and they verified, yes, a person named Luka Magnotta had lived there . . . but he had since moved on. To Russia.'

From that moment, the amateur investigation seemed to wane. Weeks and months trundled by. Magnotta had vanished off the radar. He stopped posting gratuitous pictures and videos. Activity in the *Luka_Intel* group dwindled as disheartened members departed to pursue new cases. But for Deanna, John and a handful of fellow committed sleuths, the hunt for the sadist behind the cat-killing video was far from over.

10

Unmasking Luka Magnotta

On 2 December, 2011, the video *bathtime lol* appeared online. Broadcast on a site named Flix, the video featured yet another disturbing act of extreme animal cruelty. Viewers watched with horror as a man held a petrified kitten, Sellotaped to the end of a mop handle, over a full bathtub. An up-close shot of the creature's face before being plunged to its death in the water shattered hearts all over the world. The kitten's little head and ears were a-tremble, its wide eyes glossed with terror. 'To this day, it was probably one of the worst videos I have ever seen,' recalls Deanna. 'This desperation in this cat's face that . . . it's hard to describe. It's haunting.'

Later that same day, another video titled *Python Christmas* dropped. 'My first reaction was, *"OK, this is number two."* Kind of like the feeling – not the same, but kinda like 9/11 – when the second plane hit the building . . . *"OK what's next? We're under attack."'*

The blurry footage shows the side view of a man dressed as Santa while playing with a kitten to the soundtrack of 'The Little Drummer Boy'. Santa then disappears out of shot, leaving his hat on the bed beside the feline. Next, a meaty python slinks forth from beneath the pillows and eats the cat.

Again, the 'Find the Vacuum Killer for Great Justice' page sprung to life, with members likening the perpetrator in the latest videos to Magnotta. Meanwhile, Deanna explored the origin of *Python Christmas*, published by another sock puppet account holder. The user had uploaded a black-and-white profile photograph of a young girl and had chosen the name Lesley Ann Downey. Deanna immediately recognised the name and face. The smiling girl, Lesley Ann Downey was the youngest victim of the Moors Murderers, Ian Brady and Myra Hindley. Deanna found an article online detailing Lesley's final moments at the hands of the evil couple. At Brady and Hindley's trial, the jury heard recording of Lesley pleading for her life as 'The Little Drummer Boy' plays in the background.

'The warning signs were monumental,' adds Deanna. 'This was now the second indication that Luka has a fascination for serial killers. It was very alarming.'

News of the latest kitten killings spread fast, attracting global headlines. In London, the *Sun* newspaper ran a story beneath the banner, 'Catch the sicko who fed a kitten to a python.' Following publication, The *Sun* news desk received a message. It said: 'The person you're looking for is currently in London, UK. His name is Luka Magnotta and he's staying at the Fusilier Inn. A *Sun* journalist – who'd been in touch with members of the Justice group – arranged to meet Magnotta – then secretly recorded their conversation inside a dingy bedroom at the £40-a-night Fusilier in Wembley. When asked what he was doing in London, Magnotta repeated the lies he'd fed Warmington four years ago: 'I'm here because of all the harassment. I'm getting death threats – because of the stories about me.'

The male reporter showed Magnotta a still image from *Python Christmas*. 'This is you in the picture here,' he said. 'It certainly looks like you.' Magnotta denied the lad in the Santa hat was him, adding, 'People are really good with Photoshop these days, aren't they? It's obvious, I'm being framed.'

The journalist left the room but, keen to observe Magnotta's next move, waited for a while in the hotel car park with his photographer colleague. Twenty minutes later, two plainclothes police officers arrived and escorted Magnotta away in a taxi. Unbeknownst to the reporter, the hotel manager had called the Metropolitan Police to have Magnotta evicted. Where Magnotta went next, nobody knows, but two days after his eviction from the Fusilier, the journalist received a second email and the contents would hint that the sleuths' worst fears about what Magnotta was capable of were not unfounded.

The email read:

Well, I have to say goodbye for now, but don't worry, in the near future you'll be hearing from me again. This time, however, the victims won't be small animals. I will, however, send you a copy of the new video I'm going to be making. You see, killing is different than smoking . . . with smoking you can actually quit. Once you kill, and taste, it's impossible to stop. The urge is just too strong not to continue.

You know the fun part of all this is watching millions of people get very angry and frustrated because they can't catch me. That's why I love this. I love the risk factor. It's so fun watching people work so hard gathering all the evidence, then not being able to name me or catch me. You see I always win, I always hold the trump card, and I will continue to make more movies . . . next time you hear from me it will be in a movie I'm producing. That will have some humans in it, not just pussys. :)

Well, it was fun fucking around with everyone, so have a merry Christmas and a happy new years. I know I will :) Getting away with all this, now that's genius.

Signed
Yours truly
(or is it)
John Kilbride.

John Kilbride was another victim of the Moors Murderers. Suspecting the sickening tirade had come from Magnotta, the *Sun* shared the email with the Justice group – and again alerted police. However, the Met said they couldn't arrest Magnotta as he'd made 'no direct threats to kill.' They added that the email looked to have been sent from the Netherlands, which is outside their jurisdiction.

'Scotland Yard couldn't help us,' Deanna says. 'They didn't have lawful jurisdiction. This was another stepping stone to fame [for Magnotta] – this ladder that he was building.' Fear and frustration overwhelmed the sleuthers. Magnotta had slipped through the net again. I remember somebody in our group saying, "He's going to kill somebody,"' adds John.

Soon after the chilling John Kilbride email landed, another sock puppet account posted a link to the group. The message, captioned 'Baudi Moovin 99', contained a video filmed at the casino where Deanna worked. Her heart froze as the home movie rolled on her screen. 'It was terrifying. He's [Magnotta] no longer just behind a computer. This was real. So, y'know, this [had started] off as a puzzle that I think I'm going to solve in maybe two days – get rid of some scum. And now here we are – a potential killer might be after me. I was legitimately concerned that Luka would come into my office with a knife. Or that he would somehow break into my car and be in my back seat. It was paranoia beyond rationale.'

Months slipped by and still nobody knew Magnotta's location. Had he fled to the Netherlands from London – then on to Las Vegas to stalk Deanna? Certain that Magnotta had sent the email to the *Sun*, Magnotta's words throbbed and whined in the sleuths' minds. They were certain that Magnotta would soon graduate to hurting a human being. Teetering on a precipice of nervous anticipation, the collective scoured the internet for evidence of Magnotta's whereabouts. Working as a tight unit, the investigators were relentless in their search for Magnotta.

Maia recalls: 'I searched websites for more possible instances of the kitten killer's animal cruelty or clues to suggest his location or current activity. Anything and everything that the team, or others, found was immediately shared. We tried to identify more locations from Magnotta's pictures he'd posted online. Nothing was too small to study in the minutest of detail.

'I searched every online dating and social media app, looking for Magnotta's face or aliases he might be using – and variations of those aliases. Our searches escalated to a fever pitch to track Magnotta down. As I mentioned previously, we all feared he would kill a human next. That fear intensified after the written threats.'

* * *

John Green's iPhone pinged and vibrated on his bedside table, waking him at 5 a.m. It was Saturday, 26 May, 2012. The date would mark a gruesome epitaph in John's mind.

Squinting in the muddy darkness, John reached for the phone, put on his glasses and groggily observed the alert. A

Facebook message that said, 'Hey, there's this video I just came across. I think you might want to look at it. I think it's that Luka guy you've been looking for.'

Suspecting another cat-killing video, John opened the attached 'bestgor.com' link. Beneath rapid cool breaths of the whirring ceiling fan, John pulled the duvet tight around his torso, leaned back on his propped pillows, then touched the triangle button on his screen. The depraved acts of graphic violence that erupted on John's device defied belief. He jumped out of bed and went to watch the footage on his computer screen. 'Now I'm watching it on my large monitor – and I've got it full screen. Holy shit,' he remembers.

On the screen, *1 lunatic 1 ice pick* begins. In a gloomy room, beneath a *Casablanca* poster taped to a familiar urine-coloured wall, a naked man, stretched supine on the bed. A white cloth smothers his face and his arms are spread wide in a crucifix position. His wrists are bound to the bed. New Order's 'True Faith' is playing and the camera is positioned between the victim's feet.

Seconds later, another man enters the scene. He hovers over the figure on the bed, and lightly pats his cloaked face before retreating to pick up the camera. The film then cuts to a different angle showing the suspect, dressed in black and brandishing an ice pick. The victim's head is now covered with a black sheet. His chest rises and falls, a barely discernible movement. Soon he is eclipsed by the dark figure as he hoicks his ice pick towards the ceiling, then spears it southwards, deep into the bound man's abdomen. The suspect again yanks high his weapon and, with demonic alacrity, goes on to stab his victim ninety-nine times more. 'True Faith' plays on.

The remainder of the video contains more increasingly abhorrent deeds. After his stabbing spree, the attacker hacks off his victim's arm with a knife. He masturbates with the severed limb – then uses a knife and fork to slice flesh from it. The suspect saws off the man's remaining limbs, and decapitates him. He sodomises his torso before repeating that act with a wine bottle.

Around eight minutes into the clip, the murderer places a black-and-white puppy on the bed. We hear the dog emit a small, helpless bark, before ensuing frames show the animal licking a bloodied stump of the torso.

Towards the end of the video, the killer dumps his victim's head in a bathtub, playfully swirling it in the water as though the body part were a toy. Still images charting stages of the murder – including hacked limbs assembled on the bed – conclude the harrowing ten-minute and twenty-two second film. Later, Canadian law enforcement would state that a longer version of the film strongly suggested the perpetrator had carried out acts of cannibalism on his victim.

John watched the video 'at least twenty times' that day. 'Every time I watched it, for some reason, my mind didn't want to believe it's true.' His citizen colleagues also watched the film and, while sickened and shaken by its unthinkable content, the team was in no doubt that the dark figure in the video – the murderer – was Luka Rocco Magnotta.

In *Don't F**k with Cats*, Deanna sobs as she recollects scenes from the murder video. 'It was very Luka-esque the way he petted his victim's head, like how the cat killer petted the kittens before killing them. And the background music, "True Faith", Luka had used that in his YouTube video montage. Luka likes to leave breadcrumbs.

'We were certainly worried about the human he'd killed. But why the puppy? We thought he was sending us a "Fuck you" message. Because we didn't catch him for the cat videos, he's saying, "I got away with it, now I'm graduating to a human. This dog is here as just a homage to my past."'

The sleuths' nightmare had become a heart-shattering reality. The two burning questions on their lips now were, 'Why hadn't the authorities listened to us?' and, 'Who will Luka Magnotta kill next?' They were desperate to unmask Magnotta as the killer in the video but, once more, they could not identify *where* the murder happened. So, the internet searchers again contacted detectives at Toronto Police – and emailed them their dossier of evidence. They named Luka Magnotta as the possible murderer in *1 Lunatic 1 Ice Pick*, and outlined their grave concerns that he would kill again. A day passed with radio silence. Toronto Police did not respond to the group's email. By now, *1 Lunatic 1 Ice Pick* had gone viral. Deanna set up a Google alert about the video. The amateur detectives pored over news sites, expecting to read of the discovery of body parts somewhere. They found no such reports.

'The thing that kept us on edge and frayed our nerves was simply trying to figure out what he would do next,' explains Maia. 'Where would he pop up next? We had a desperate need to find him, stop him – before he killed another animal or human.'

As time passed, still without answers, Deanna again feared Magnotta might target her. 'We didn't know what he was going to do next. We felt we had a ticking time bomb on our hands, and we wanted it to stop. Now, I'm scared to death. Is he going to come after me now? I mean, he knows where I work.'

In the face of her terror, Deanna opened her laptop and carried on sleuthing. She returned to Magnotta's vainglorious YouTube slideshows, pausing the screen to examine each photograph in the hope of finding just one pointer that would reveal his whereabouts.

During her search, Deanna stumbled across a new Magnotta YouTube video. It displayed many of the same images featured in his other slideshows – Magnotta's head on other people's bodies in pictures shot in exotic locations. It was nothing Deanna hadn't seen before – until, halfway through the video, a new image of Magnotta appeared. Instantly, Deanna knew the picture was not one of Magnotta's photoshopped efforts. There were no awkward lines or clashes in skin colour and the landscape looked genuine too. The picture presented Magnotta, in lilac trousers and a royal blue T-shirt, leaning against a drystone wall abutting rocky steps. Zooming in on the picture, Deanna spotted vital clues in its backdrop: a tree sprouting spring buds, an arced streetlight and, most importantly, a set of traffic lights – they were black and boxy, unlike the buttercupcoloured stoplights found in Toronto. Searching Google images, Deanna found a set of lights that matched those in Magnotta's photograph. Clicking on the image took her to a news article whose headline would prove pivotal to the amateurs' probe: 'Should Montrealers be allowed to drive through red lights?'

'The hairs immediately went up on the back of my neck,' says Deanna. 'I thought, *"Oh my God, maybe he went to Montreal."*'

Deanna messaged John, who had also found the new Magnotta picture, and the pair began the painstaking job of digitally navigating the streets of Montreal on Google Street View. 'We're literally going through Street View, step, by step, by step,' says John in *Don't F**k with Cats*. 'She's [Deanna] going down one street, I'm going down another street. Then, all of a sudden, we go, "Holy shit" – there's the stairs, right over there.' The duo had found the exact spot from the photograph: the steps in front of McGill University in Downtown Montreal. Their revelation coincided with breaking news. It was the bulletin they'd morbidly been expecting: a man's torso had been found in rubbish in a Montreal alley.

Furious comments flooded the *Find the Kitten Vacuumer* Facebook page. After seventeen months' hard work culminating in their message to Toronto Police – Magnotta had done what they had all feared he would do. Group members were understandably devastated. Why had nobody listened to them? The team forwarded their findings on Luka Magnotta to Montreal Police. Again, they received no response.

A bilious tangle of emotions consumed Deanna: grief for the murdered man and his family, rage at the authorities who had not listened, fear, anger and repugnance as flashbacks of *1 Lunatic, 1 Ice Pick* plagued her. Then, a fog of guilt enveloped her and she subsequently left the Facebook groups.

Deanna explains in the documentary: 'You go through this spectrum of blame, blaming yourself – and it makes you sick. Your stomach hurts and you're throwing up. You're not eating.

'I just wanted to crawl up in bed with my dogs and watch bad reality TV. So, I needed to go off-grid.'

In Montreal, the police investigation got underway. A forensic tent covered the site where the janitor had found the maggot-infested suitcase among the refuse as media crews thronged around the cordoned crime scene.

Examining the blood-pooled rubbish that smelled of death, forensic detectives unearthed a wine bottle, a crumpled *Casablanca* poster, and a dead black-and-white puppy. Severed limbs, minus their hands and feet were found decomposing in the debris. One bin sack contained blood-drenched blankets. In another bag, they found paperwork – an Ontario driving licence and a pharmacy receipt. Both items bore the name, Luka Rocco Magnotta, complete with his address: apartment 208, 5720 Decarie Boulevard, Montreal. At that stage, police thought Magnotta might be the victim.

A sharp smell engulfed officers when they entered apartment 208. Metallic and rotten but also bleachy – it was the aroma of blood cutting through a haze of cleaning fluids. Small and dingy, the apartment's main room trebled as a kitchen, lounge and bedroom. The double bed was squished between a radiator and a gaudy velour two-seater sofa All the blinds and curtains were closed. The place was silent and bare, the only evidence of recent occupation being a half-drunk bottle of lemon juice and a brown fitted sheet scruffily hugging the mattress.

On the surface, the apartment looked clean, but forensic tests would soon reveal the horrors that occurred in apartment 208. Detective Sergeant Claudette Hamlin said the bed alone 'lit up like a discotheque' when treated with luminol — a chemical that glows when it reacts with blood. Traces of blood were also discovered in the refrigerator and bath. A message, inked in red pen inside a cupboard, warned: 'If you don't like the reflection, don't look in the mirror. I don't care.'

A friend of Jun Lin identified his body as an arrest warrant was issued for Magnotta, who'd already fled the country. Two weeks after his arrest in Berlin, Magnotta was flown back to Canada aboard a military jet.

Magnotta's trial started in September 2014 and lasted ten weeks. He admitted killing Jun Lin and dismembering his body before posting parts to politicians and schools — but claimed diminished responsibility due to mental health disorders. During the trial jurors were shown the *1 Lunatic 1 Ice Pick* video, as well graphic photographs depicting Magnotta's blood-soaked flat after he slaughtered his victim.

The prosecution said Magnotta had hatched his plan to film himself killing a human at least six months before Jun was butchered. But Magnotta's lawyer, Luc Leclair argued his client was in a psychotic state and 'unable to tell right from wrong' when he killed Jun.

The jury spent eight days deliberating before returning a guilty verdict on all charges against the depraved killer on 23 December, 2014. He was given an automatic life sentence for first-degree murder, with no possibility of parole for twenty-five years. He was sentenced to a further nineteen years for the four other charges, including distributing obscene materials and indignities to a human body.

* * *

Luka Magnotta clearly adored being chased by the online detective groups. Did this attention fuel Magnotta's murderous mind? As Deanne says in *Don't F**k with Cats*, 'I wonder, did I do too much? I asked myself, *"Did you egg him on?"* And it [the attention from those searching for him] was just like a drug? It stopped being enough for him. Did he need more?'

Mark Mendelson, a retired Toronto Police Service homicide detective, says killing Jun Lin was probably the 'next logical step' for Magnotta. He tells me, 'You can't get inside Magnotta's head – and Lord knows, you wouldn't want to. People like Magnotta have a psychological need to feed their obsession. In a way, it isn't much different to a drug addict – when they reach the point when the substance they're taking doesn't give them the same high that it used to, they take more. Magnotta performs this cruelty to animals, and he gets great shock value on the internet for it – and that's gratifying for him, whether it's in a sexual way or not.

'At its lowest level, how many cats do you have to kill before you move on? You're sending out a clip of you doing things to cats and dogs and eventually you're not going to get the same reaction from that online community, so you need to go one step bigger.

'Let's face it, Magnotta took a huge step. He went to cannibalism for God's sake, and he filmed that. And he mailed body parts. So this is all part of his need to be recognised, feared and admired. And at the end of the day, it's all "Catch me if you can. I dare you".'

Mark now runs a private investigation firm and frequently appears on Canadian television as a crime expert. He spent fourteen years as a lead homicide investigator, overseeing dozens of gruesome murder cases, but even he was shocked when he watched Magnotta's *1 Lunatic 1 Ice pick*. 'After Magnotta's trial, I did two hours or so straight television interviews about the case, so I watched the video. And I would say, as a seasoned detective, it blew me out of my chair. I remember thinking, '*Is he really doing that?*'

'I've had a couple of murders where people have dismembered their victim and, in some cases, started cooking them. And the common theme I noticed when interviewing those murderers is that they did not realise how much work was involved. They complain about the effort it takes to chop a body up. "Man, that was hard work," one killer said to me, still covered in blood. Whereas Magnotta did it with a grin on his face. If Magnotta hadn't been caught in that internet café in Berlin, I absolutely believe he would have killed another person . . . soon.'

11

The 'Lord' of Bioinformatics

Stateville Correctional Center, Illinois, 10 May, 1994, 12.01 a.m.

Approaching 'Killer Clown' John Wayne Gacy on the gurney in the execution chamber, warden Sal Godinez asked him, 'Do you have any final words?'

Gacy rolled his head towards the curtained window, beyond which twenty-four witnesses sat – there to watch the killer die by lethal injection – then he looked up at Godinez. Gacy's meaty face shone with sweat, his hands still greasy from his last meal – a bucket of original recipe KFC chicken, French fries, a dozen fried shrimps and a pound of strawberries. His expression flicked from a grin to a sneer as he expelled his final three words. 'Kiss my ass.'

Paramedics hooked Gacy up to a heart monitor and an IV drip. One of two executioners would administer three injections – first, midazolam, to knock him unconscious. The second jab, vecuronium bromide, would stop him from breathing, and a final dose of potassium chloride would stop his heart.

At 12.40 a.m. the curtains parted, revealing Gacy's final audience. The two executioners took their positions at the lethal injection machine behind a one-way mirror. Then, on Godinez's signal, they both pressed a button to release the deadly drugs.

The solution flowed and pumped into Gacy's veins, beginning the execution of the fifty-two-year-old prisoner who'd spent fourteen years on Death Row. But then a problem occurred when the second chemical 'gelled' and clogged the IV tube. The tube had to be replaced, which delayed Gacy's passing. He was eventually pronounced dead at 12.58 a.m. – as a thousand-strong crowd of celebrators thronged outside the prison, brandishing banners and chanting, 'Goodbye Gacy' to the tune of 'Hello Dolly'.

William Kunkle, chief prosecutor in Gacy's trial, said after the execution, 'He got a much easier death than all of his victims. In my opinion, he got a much easier death than he deserved.'

John Wayne Gacy sexually assaulted, tortured and killed at least thirty-three boys and young men between 1972 and 1978 in Cook County, Illinois. He would trick them into entering his home using his reputation as a local businessman and respected member of the community. Gacy ran a successful building and decorating company, was a well-liked neighbour and worked with the local branch of the Democratic Party. The serial killer often performed as a clown – he had two personas 'Pogo' and 'Patches' at charity events and children's hospitals. Photographs of Gacy in his frilly costume with his bloated face painted red, white and blue conjure terrifying images now we understand the depths of his depravity. It is unsurprising to learn that Gacy was Stephen King's inspiration for the demonic clown, Pennywise, in his horror novel, *IT*.

After luring his victims into his house, Gacy would tell the young men he was going to perform a magic trick on them, convincing them to put on handcuffs as part of the game. There was no magic trick – and once Gacy had them bound, he raped and killed them before ditching their bodies in lime in a shallow crawl space beneath his house or later dumping his victims in the local Des Plaines River. Most of Gacy's victims were strangled or choked.

Just before his arrest in December 1978, Gacy made a drunk, rambling statement to his lawyer Sam Amirante, admitting that he'd tortured, raped and killed dozens of young men. During this confession, which Gacy would later try to retract, he told Amirante how he'd buried most of his victims in his crawl space and dumped a further five of his victims in the Des Plaines River. Gacy said he sometimes woke to find 'dead, strangled kids' in his home. 'I was going to put a second storey on my house − because I ran out of room for the bodies,' he said during his confession.

Investigators subsequently unearthed the remains of twenty-nine bodies on the torturer's property and a further four were found in the rivers south-east of Chicago. Gacy never showed any remorse or empathy for his victims. Even facing his own death, he chose not to apologise for his atrocious crimes and instead further insulted his victims' grieving loved ones with his snarling and defiant last words.

Gacy's body was cremated and his sister from Arkansas claimed the ashes, but his brain was removed first with her permission. The organ was given to Chicago-based psychiatrist, Dr Helen Morrison, who had testified for the defence at Gacy's 1980 trial. She had claimed that the serial killer was mentally ill and legally insane. Dr Morrison had his brain examined by scientists at the University of Chicago Medical Center − she wanted to see if it contained any abnormalities that might possibly explain his warped desires to kill. However, experts could find nothing wrong with Gacy's brain. 'There was no tumour, no growth, no sign of an injury. The ventricles are fine; no sign of hydrocephalus,' Dr Morrison concluded.

And, no amount of examination of Gacy's brain would reveal the names of eight of his victims who remained unidentified when he was executed. Their skeletal remains were buried with their true names still unknown. Some of the killer's victims were runaways, estranged from their families and making their way through the world alone – and so were not reported as missing at the time.

By 2011, advances in DNA technology meant that law enforcement could try to provide answers for some of those victims' families. That year, the Cook County's Sheriff Department exhumed the eight nameless men and appealed for anyone with a male relative who had disappeared during Gacy's killing spree in the seventies to submit a DNA sample. The response was overwhelming, and, within weeks, Sheriff Tom Dart revealed one set of remains had been identified.

The victim was nineteen-year-old construction worker William Bundy, previously known as Victim No. 19 (the identifier given to him because he was the nineteenth victim removed from Gacy's crawl space). His brother, Robert, and sister, Laura O'Leary, provided saliva samples, which scientists at the University of North Texas then matched to William's DNA. At the time of the discovery, Laura told the *Associated Press* how she'd always suspected that Gacy killed her brother. She said the family had filed a missing person's report for William when he vanished in Chicago in October 1976. When the bodies were found in Gacy's home, the only way of identifying their brother would have been through dental records. But their dentist had since retired and destroyed all his records. Determining whether one of the bodies in the crawlspace was William Bundy was impossible.

'Today's terribly sad,' said Laura upon William's identification in November 2011. 'But it is also a day that provides closure. We have been waiting a long time for closure.'

Six years later, another family would discover how their missing loved one also fell prey to Gacy. In July 2017, Victim No. 24 was identified as sixteen-year-old Jimmy Haakenson, a 'good-natured but troubled' lad who ran away from his Minnesota home in August 1976. Jimmy fled to Chicago then called his mother, June Haakenson to say he'd arrived and assured her, 'I'm safe, I'm here, Mom. Don't worry.' Those would be the last words Jimmy said to June, who sadly died in 2005 without ever knowing what happened to her son.

A DNA sample supplied by Jimmy's sister, Lorie Sisterman, meant authorities could identify Jimmy's remains. Lorie said the family had long wondered whether her brother had been a Gacy victim. 'One of the worst people in the world who walked the earth murdered my brother,' she said at the time. 'You hope for something different, but I'm so glad to know where my brother is.'

Another significant breakthrough came in October 2021 when forensic genealogists at the DNA Doe Project identified Victim No. 5 as Francis Wayne Alexander, from North Carolina. The long journey to identify Francis began when DNA was extracted from one of Victim No. 5's molars. The molar DNA was sent away for sequencing by experts at the HudsonAlpha Institute for Biotechnology in Huntsville, Alabama. Coordinating this process was a Texas-based engineer and genetics sleuth, Kevin Lord, who kindly agreed to meet me online to talk about his work with the project.

Kevin holds a unique role within the DNA Doe Project and he laughs when he recites his title. 'I'm director of lab and agency logistics at the DNA Doe Project, which is quite a lengthy title,' he says, rubbing his coarse raven beard. 'Basically, I'm the main point of contact with all the agencies at the beginning of an investigation.

'I talk to sheriffs' and coroners' offices and figure out what human remains they have available. I'll ask whether they have blood from an autopsy, or bones, teeth, hair or tissue samples. I try to determine what is going to be the best route to get the DNA that we need for the sequencing – then I work with them to get the DNA sent off to our various partner laboratories, where they'll extract the DNA before sending it on to a sequencing lab.'

The sequenced DNA consists of a massive, compressed text file detailing base-pairings of ACTG (an acronym for the four bases found in a DNA molecule – adenine, cytosine, thymine and guanine). This file is then returned to Kevin, who works his bioinformatics magic on the raw data through his company, Saber Investigations, which specialises in genetic genealogy techniques. Bioinformatics is the science of storing, retrieving and analysing large amounts of biological data – and Kevin is well regarded for his mastery of the science. 'We call Kevin the Lord of Bioinformatics,' his colleague at DNA Doe Project, Tracie Boyle told me. 'He's a whizz at all that stuff.'

The process sounds mind-blowing to me as Kevin explains it. 'Each sequencing read will have a bunch of ACTG in whatever combination for 150 bases long,' Kevin explains. 'Additionally, there will be some metadata in there, explaining how confident each base is, and information about the sequencing read – but it's just little individual fragments.

'There's a bunch of different steps on the bioinformatics side of things, but the main one is to look at the individual readings and try to line them up with where they fit along the human genome. Once we have a profile – an edited subset of the massive sequence file – it can be uploaded to the genealogy site GEDmatch.com, which allows users to upload their DNA samples from competing companies like Ancestry.com and 23andMe to be compared.'

Obtaining a strong DNA profile is dependent on the quality of the sample provided, and this was a challenge when it came to the remains of Victim No. 5. The DDP was 'lucky' to have a clean molar tooth to work with, says Kevin.

'If I had any choice of a sample, a blood card is going to be the best. Nowadays, if a victim is unidentified, the pathologist will take a blood sample and drop it onto a card. This stabilises and preserves the DNA. The card is then stored at room temperature and kept on file. Obviously, this option wasn't available in Francis's case as the remains were skeletal, dating back to the seventies. Blood cards are rarely available from unidentified victims from the early two-thousands even. When blood isn't available, a tooth is the next best thing, especially a molar tooth with no cavities or dental work. So, we were lucky there was a molar for Francis.'

Once a strong DNA profile had been established for Victim No. 5 and uploaded to GEDmatch.com, it took the DDP team just eight hours to identify him.

'With traditional DNA testing that was used years ago, a close DNA match was needed – a parent for example,' says Kevin, who was also a volunteer team leader in the case. 'But now we can make a match via the victim's second, third, fourth or fifth cousins. In Francis's case, we got lucky and found a second cousin through his maternal great grandparents. Second cousins are great – they share just over three per cent DNA. We also found a third and a fifth cousin, both once removed, on the paternal side of Francis's family.'

The genealogists then ran the three cousins' names through online public records, social media and news archives and eventually connected Victim No. 5 with Francis Wayne Alexander.

'Yeah, we were lucky,' adds Kevin. 'We got our match quickly and presented our findings to the sheriff's office the next day.' DNA swabs later provided by Francis's surviving relatives matched Victim No. 5's genetic sample.

On 25 October, 2021, thanks to the dedicated work of the DDP team, Cook County Sheriff Tom Dart could finally announce to the world the latest revelation in the ongoing search for the identities of Gacy's unnamed victims. He said Francis would have been twenty-one or twenty-two when Gacy killed him sometime between January 1976 and early 1977. He added that the news had come as a huge shock to Francis's family, who thought he'd 'just wanted to be left alone' after moving from his home state in the early seventies.

Displayed on a board at the press conference were three photographs of Francis beneath his name and the text: 'Located December 1978. Identified October 2021.' One picture showed Francis as a young boy at a wedding, dressed smartly with a short, pudding-basin haircut and a sharp white carnation pinned to the lapel of his blazer. His smile is wide and proud. Another image was of Francis as a teenager, his expression a little more serious, with his bronze wavy hair styled in a Hollywood-inspired side parting. And the final, and most poignant image was one of the last known photographs taken of Francis, possibly not long before Gacy killed him. In this picture he looks just as pristine as usual and is sporting a neat moustache, a white, ruffled dress shirt and black bow tie. His smile, is still, wide and proud.

Dart shared what he'd gleaned about Francis's life and movements prior to his murder. Francis was born in North Carolina but moved to New York, where he married a young woman. The newlyweds relocated to Chicago in 1975 but divorced around three months later. Dart said that it's not known how Francis crossed paths with Gacy but confirmed that the victim lived in an area of Chicago frequented by the serial killer. In January 1976, Francis received a traffic ticket, but officers found no record of him thereafter.

In a statement read by the sheriff, Francis's family said: 'It is hard, even forty-five years later, to know the fate of our beloved

Wayne. He was killed at the hands of a vile and evil man. Our hearts are heavy. Our sympathies go out to other victims' families. Our only comfort is knowing this killer no longer breathes the same air as we do. We can now lay to rest what happened and move forward by honouring Wayne.'

The DDP, with Cook County Sheriff Office, is now working to identify Gacy's remaining five unidentified victims from DNA profiles obtained from their remains.

* * *

Kevin tells me that he began delving into cold cases five years ago when a 'burnout' finally convinced him to leave his previous programming job in the tech industry. He took things easy for a while, set up a business selling T-shirts on Amazon, and watched back-to-back episodes of what had become his new obsession: *Disappeared*. It was this Investigation Discovery documentary series, chronicling missing person cases in America, that inspired Kevin to investigate the separate disappearances of two women from where he lived in Killeen, Texas. He cast his net wide, filed records requests with law enforcement agencies in the area, pored over court documents and arrest reports and interviewed friends and relatives of the missing women. But it was when he tried linking the two women to unidentified bodies, that he stumbled upon Lavender Doe.

She was named Lavender Doe because of the lilac jumper she had on when two men found her corpse, face down on a blazing bonfire in woods near Longview, Texas on 29 October, 2006. The men, who were out target shooting when they noticed the burning figure, initially thought she was a mannequin – set alight by Halloween pranksters, perhaps. But the fumes from the fire were not indicative of burning rubber. The smell was one of stale hotdogs cooking on charcoal and cutting through were sharp wafts of gasoline. Flames jumped, curled and cracked around the figure. Approaching the blaze, the target shooters glimpsed her legs, sheathed in denim. They then spotted an empty petrol can, resting on its side in a bed of leaves next to the fire. They coughed on the air. as the horrific realisation hit them that the smell was burning flesh and gasoline and the figure on the bonfire was a human – a woman – and she was most certainly dead. She had been doused in gasoline, set ablaze and left to burn in her lavender sweater.

Gregg County Sheriff's Office established only a few physical details about the victim, as her body and face were burned beyond recognition. She was estimated to be between seventeen and twenty-five, around eight stone, with strawberry blonde hair. One notable feature, however, was the woman's perfect teeth and the fact that she still had two milk teeth, which was unusual for her age. Investigators hoped dental records might identify the victim. Some clothing was recovered – the scorched lavender jumper and a pair of jeans branded 'One Tuff Babe', with forty dollars stuffed in one pocket. Semen was found inside the woman and at the murder scene, prompting detectives to believe her killer had also raped her. But despite police and media appeals to identify the victim, no one came forward with information. Even a clay bust reconstruction of the woman didn't trigger a response from the public. DNA samples taken from the charred corpse were compared to the genetic profiles of missing women, but none of them matched.

The victim was buried in White Cemetery, east Texas, under a 'Jane Doe' grave marker. Her killer was then still unknown. However, a suspect emerged in 2007 when detectives matched the semen found inside the victim to thirty-six-year-old sex offender Joseph Burnette, who was in jail for another crime. During interview, Burnette admitted having sex with a woman but denied murdering her. He didn't know the woman's name, he said.

Six years later, in a further push to identify the woman who had been burned to death, law enforcement exhumed her body from the small cemetery. The National Center for Missing and Exploited Children (NCMEC) joined the investigation. Carl Koppelman created a three-dimensional facial reconstruction to demonstrate how the victim might have appeared during life. Again, the rendering wasn't recognised by anyone.

By now, armchair sleuths had fully immersed themselves in the Lavender Doe murder case – examining the gruesome killing in minute detail and asking pertinent questions. Was she already dead before being burned? Or was she burned alive? Did the victim know her killer? And, most importantly, who was she? They tried to link the victim to reported missing women of a similar age and description and sent their suggestions to the NCMEC. It was when those names were rejected as matches, that a Websleuths member christened the woman 'Lavender Doe', a moniker that was quickly propagated by the media and local community.

When Kevin found the Lavender Doe thread on Websleuths, he was intrigued by the thirty-plus pages of comments about the woman's 'perfect smile' and suggested theories surrounding her death. Soon, he was hooked by the mystery of who this woman had been. 'At first, I suspected Lavender Doe might be one of the two missing women I'd been trying to locate – because she had distinctive teeth,' he says. 'I became totally obsessed with the Lavender Doe case. I dived headfirst into it.'

Eventually, believing he might have a name for the mystery woman, Kevin contacted Gregg County Sheriff's Office and spoke with the lead detective in the Lavender Doe investigation,

Lieutenant Eddie Hope. The enigma had consumed Eddie for eleven years. During that time, he frequently visited Lavender Doe's grave.

With all clues exhausted, Eddie welcomed Kevin's call, touched that a member of the public wanted to help find a name for Lavender Doe. Unfortunately, the first missing woman Kevin suggested for the victim had already been eliminated as a match, but Eddie urged him to call back with any new tips. 'I was like a dog with a bone then,' recalls Kevin. 'I continued to dig for clues. I'd be glued to my computer for hours, searching missing person listings and social media accounts, delving into more court records and police files. I started contributing to the Lavender Doe thread on Websleuths – and another conversation on the topic on a Reddit forum. This kind of work felt like my calling, so I signed up for a course to become a licensed private investigator.'

The course required Kevin to complete an externship (form of training also known as an internship) – and he knew of an organisation that would be the perfect fit for his placement. He'd long been interested in genealogy and had followed the DNA DOE Project (DDP) on Facebook. It was April 2018, and the DDP had just announced its first solved case. Working with law enforcement and the Miami Valley Regional Crime Laboratory, DDP volunteers had helped identify a woman who had been found stabbed and strangled to death in a ditch in Ohio in 1981. Until now, the victim had been known only as Buckskin Girl – because she was wearing a fringed deerskin poncho. The breakthrough came via Buckskin Girl's DNA obtained from a blood sample that had lain in storage for over three decades. Armed with this genetic data, the DDP successfully matched it to a sample submitted by a first cousin, which led to the identification of the victim: twenty-one-year-old Marcia King, from Arkansas.

Kevin points out that this was the first cold case to be solved with genetic genealogy that the world learned about. Buckskin Girl's real name was announced to the public on 10 April – two weeks before Paul Holes unmasked Joseph DeAngelo as the Golden State Killer. The solving of both cases verified the power of genetic genealogy as an investigative crime-busting tool – and as a method Kevin believed could also proffer a name for Lavender Doe. He approached DDP co-founder, Margaret Press. She was impressed with Kevin's tech background and ancestry investigation skills – he'd recently researched his family tree to centuries back – and immediately snapped him up. That summer, the DDP crowdfunded $1,400 to analyse Lavender Doe's DNA – and Kevin would lead the investigation.

Around this time in 2018, Gregg County Sheriff's Office announced a major development in the Lavender Doe murder inquiry. Eddie Hope and his colleagues had discovered another woman's body, dumped in the woods in Longview. Eddie had noticed her purple fingernails poking through the maple leaves that blanketed her corpse. This time, Eddie had a name for the murder victim. She was Felisha Pearson, the girlfriend of Joseph Burnette, who'd been released from prison the previous year.

Felisha's mother had reported her missing, naming Burnette as the last person seen with her daughter. Police had another good reason to arrest him as he'd failed to register as a sex offender upon release. Under questioning, Burnette casually confessed to strangling Felisha with a rope. And when detectives again quizzed him about Lavender Doe's murder, Burnette finally gave a bored snigger and replied: 'Yeah, I did the same to her. I killed her too.' Burnette then told officers how he'd murdered Lavender Doe.

He said it was because she 'stole money' from him. She'd approached him outside a Walmart store in Longview, he said, where she was selling items from a brochure. Burnette claimed he convinced Lavender Doe to get into his truck with him. 'She tried to sell me lingerie out of a magazine. I didn't want that. She agreed to have sex with me – then she stole my money,' said Burnette. 'So, I took her to the woods and put a rope around her neck. I choked her – it only took seconds. I set her on fire then I left. I left forty dollars in her pocket that was money she'd earned.' Burnette said he thought the woman's name might have been Ashley.

Burnette was charged with both murders, but, despite his confessions, he pleaded not guilty at his first court hearing. The DDP team now faced the challenge of tracing the identity of the victim labelled Lavender Doe in court papers – before Burnette's trial.

Joining Kevin on his mission to win justice for Lavender Doe were fellow volunteers: Missy Koski, a 'search angel' who helps reunite adoptees with their birth parents; and genealogy enthusiast Lori Gaff. Throughout the stifling Texan summer, the trio worked day and night from their bedrooms, basements and living rooms – meeting online to discuss their progress. 'I'd sit down at my computer and one hour would suddenly become ten hours,' says Kevin. 'Sometimes, all three of us worked right through the night. I had to know everything about this case. Strange though it may sound, I felt as though I knew Lavender Doe. She had become a part of me, and I couldn't let her go. We had to find a name for her.'

Lavender Doe's DNA returned thousands of matches on the GEDmatch database, most of which were too distant to pursue. But there did appear to be a handful of third and fourth cousins and a second cousin once removed. Starting with the closer matches, the volunteers began building family trees and quickly established that Lavender had Czech ancestors. They then found baptism records in the original Czech, which enabled them to link two of Lavender's distant relatives. Searching for descendants of those ancestors, Kevin came across a woman in her late fifties who lived in east Texas – just thirty miles from the oilfield murder scene. Finding relatives who live in the area where an unclaimed body is found can be a huge clue, explains Kevin. 'It seemed it would be a huge coincidence if this woman in east Texas *wasn't* related to Lavender Doe. When I found her, I thought, "*This is it, I've found Lavender Doe's mum.*" It just felt right.'

Buoyed by his discovery, Kevin alerted Eddie, who drove out to meet the woman, hopeful for answers. But the descendent Kevin suspected to be Lavender's mother recoiled in shock when greeted by the cowboy-hatted cop on her doorstep. 'I don't know of a missing person in my family,' she said. 'I don't know who this woman could be. How can somebody *not* know that their relative has disappeared?'

Kevin's immediate reaction to the revelation was to suspect the woman was lying. The family tree proved her connection with Lavender Doe's ancestors, and geographically she was in the right place at the right time. Then another thought crossed Kevin's mind: '*Maybe this woman doesn't know she's related to Lavender.*'

Eddie returned to see the woman again. This time, he explained to her the complicated familial puzzle the genealogists were trying to unravel, and she agreed to help. She had recently taken a DNA test and would share her results with the DDP. The GEDmatch outcome astonished her – she shared enough DNA with Lavender Doe to make them first cousins once removed. Lavender Doe was probably a daughter of one of the woman's first cousins. The next step was logical. Kevin and his colleagues just needed to find the right cousin – one with a missing daughter.

But as Kevin tells me, this task was not as straightforward as it sounds: 'There were twenty-seven first cousins who could have been Lavender Doe's parent, so we started to research every person in this family. We pulled hundreds of threads, many of which led nowhere. And then I found Robin, a cousin of the east Texas woman.'

The east Texas woman knew nothing about Robin, her uncle's daughter from a previous marriage. But instinct told Kevin that this unknown cousin could be the key to giving Lavender Doe her name back. Gradually, the pieces of the jigsaw began to shuffle into place. Kevin found a death certificate for Robin, who died, aged fifty, in Indiana a month before Lavender Doe was killed. The volunteers pieced together a dossier on Robin based on information gleaned from police records and newspaper reports that revealed her many arrests for alcohol-related offences. They ran Robin's name through people-finder databases, social media sites and family records, where they found marriage certificates for two ex-husbands. There was no record of children born from those partnerships, but it seemed Robin had married a third time – she had acquired a new surname, Dodd, in some newspaper articles. Kevin googled the name which led him to a people-finder site that logged Robin as living with a man called Johnny Dodd. 'I realised this was a tenuous link but definitely worth looking into. I found Johnny Dodd – and subsequently learned that he and Robin had a daughter who, if alive, would be was around Lavender Doe's age.'

Kevin typed the daughter's name, Dana Lynn Dodd, into the private investigators' database, Delvepoint, then gawked at the result on the screen. His arms broke out in goosebumps, his mouth gaped as he pitched forward in his seat. The text revealed Dana's social security number – and it had been inactive since 2006. 'Dana had dropped off the map in the same year that Lavender Doe was found dead,' says Kevin. 'There were addresses listed for Dana up until 2006 but nothing after then. She'd vanished.'

Although Kevin did find an old MySpace page for a Dana Lynn Dodd. He couldn't be sure whether the account belonged to the same Dana who'd disappeared from government records, but she looked familiar to him. Like the woman portrayed in Carl Koppelman's recent digital reconstruction of Lavender Doe, he thought. Dana had strawberry blonde hair that fell just below her shoulders, blue eyes and a buoyant smile that showcased her perfect teeth. '*This must be Lavender Doe.*' He searched for a death certificate for Dana, but one didn't exist. Robin died before her daughter disappeared and she had no other children, but Johnny Dodd had other kids from another marriage in Jacksonville, Florida. One of those children was Amanda Gadd, Dana's half-sister. Records showed that Amanda, nine years older than Dana, still lived in Jacksonville and had children. Amanda's phone number was also listed. Kevin emailed his newfound evidence to his teammates. 'Could Dana Dodd be Lavender Doe?' he wrote.

Eddie, being the official detective in the investigation, called Amanda that same day. Naturally, she was devastated to hear her sister's name connected to a murder victim who'd rested unnamed in a lonely cemetery for the last twelve years. Amanda painted a sad picture of Dana's troubled upbringing. Abandoned as a baby by both parents, Dana was shunted from home to home before her stepmother in Arizona took her in. But when Dana turned fourteen, the stepmother sent her to Florida to live with Amanda. A rebellious teenager, Dana started taking drugs and got into trouble with the police for fighting and underage smoking. Amanda told Eddie that Dana left town with a boyfriend in 2000. Three years later, relatives started filing missing person reports for Dana, she said.

When Eddie raised the DNA testing idea, Amanda readily agreed to provide a sample. She was hoping that her genetic make-up didn't mirror that of tragic Lavender Doe because she wanted to believe Dana was alive, that she'd simply moved on and had lost touch with her family. In early December 2018, Amanda submitted her DNA swab to the lab. She and the investigating team would endure a six-week wait for the results.

'Oh, that was a long winter,' says Kevin, lifting his chunky brows. 'Missy, Lori, Eddie and I had spent months working on this project. We'd exchanged hundreds of messages, shared our revelations and now, it was a waiting game. And we knew the outcome would be sad: if Amanda's test didn't match Lavender Doe's, we would still have an unnamed murder victim, and if the two women's DNA profiles did match, then we would need to break that upsetting news to Amanda. For every solve, a family is left in mourning.'

A covering of frost smothered the grounds of White Cemetery on the morning of 29 January, 2019. Overnight, the temperature had dipped to minus three degress centigrade, icing the purple irises resting upon the small stone engraved 'Jane Doe' to a fitting shade of violet. There were always flowers at Lavender Doe's grave – bouquets left by locals who would never forget the unnamed victim who'd become part of their community.

Later that day, long after the frost had melted, Kevin heard back from the lab. The result from Amanda's genetic sample had landed and it revealed that her DNA matched that of Lavender Doe. They finally had a name for the face in the artists' sketches: Dana Lynn Dodd, the woman with the baby-toothed smile, killed seven weeks after her twenty-first birthday.

Once again, the DDP volunteers' talents and hard work had prevailed. Thanks to the amateur sleuths, the murder victim could be laid to rest with her real name engraved on her headstone. But, as Kevin acknowledged, such victories are invariably weighted with sadness. 'We felt a mixture of emotions,' he adds. 'While happy that we'd identified Dana as the victim, our success meant her family was now in mourning.'

The DDP announced Lavender Doe's identity on 11 February, 2019 – before Burnette's murder trial. Following this, details of Dana's last known steps emerged. After fleeing Florida in 2000, Dana arrived in Texas, where she joined a magazine sales team run by a violent human trafficking gang who lured employees with the promise of travel opportunities and bonuses. Workers were denied food and beaten for not meeting sales targets, it's alleged. Dana had been soliciting customers in the Walmart car park in Longview when she got into Burnette's truck.

Dana's family, so grateful to those who found her and the Longview residents who looked after her, decided she should remain in White Cemetery. 'Dana needed to be here because she is part of Longview's family,' Amanda told reporters at the memorial on the day her sister was returned to the grave. 'Now, it's all about justice for Dana.'

In December 2020, Joseph Burnette changed his plea to guilty for the murders of Dana Lynn Dodd and Felisha Pearson. He cut a bloated figure in the dock, his lardy hips and middle accentuated by the horizontal black stripes circling his prison-issue jumpsuit. The double killer didn't even flinch when the judge sentenced him to fifty years for each slaying. However, his sentences are concurrent, meaning Burnette will be sixty-five when eligible for parole in July 2043.

Lavender Doe and Gacy's Victim No. 5 are just two of the DDP's prominent cases Kevin has helped to solve. As the bioinformatics man, Kevin is involved in every investigation assigned to the DDP, juggling his lab work with genealogy research. His latest endeavour has led him full circle back to Gregg County, where he's again joined forces with Lieutenant Eddie Hope on another cold case. She's known as Gregg County Jane Doe 2002, named after the year that construction workers found her skeletal remains off Highway 135 in the Gladewater area. The victim is aged between eighteen and thirty and has a distinguishing feature: an unrepaired cleft palate. 'We managed to obtain DNA from the Doe's bones and that sample was sequenced in December 2020,' explains Kevin. 'We have some good matches and we're currently building out family trees.' But, like most Doe mystery investigations, challenges exist – and in this case, an endogamic 'tangle' has presented itself. 'This is when a lot of people from a small population have married within that population over many years, which makes it difficult to establish how people are related to one another,' Kevin explains.

Based on the family trees, Kevin believes that Gregg County Jane Doe 2002 is from the mountainous regions of West Virginia or North Carolina. 'It's a tricky one – our genealogy team has been working on this Jane Doe case for over a year now – but I'm confident we'll find a name for her. We'll keep plugging away until we do.'

12

When Sleuthing Goes Wrong

**Sheraton Boston Hotel, City of Boston,
Thursday, 18 April, 2013, 5 p.m.**

A chattering of camera mirrors welcomes Boston's FBI chief Rick DesLauriers as he steps up to a lectern almost hidden by microphones. Face taut, he gestures left, at the pair of easels displaying various photographs of two young men in baseball caps whom DesLauriers names 'Suspect 1' and 'Suspect 2'. The duo was caught on camera in the Massachusetts capital three days ago, the special agent tells his audience, when two bombs exploded near the finishing line of the annual Boston Marathon, killing three people and injuring two hundred and sixty others. DesLauriers believes Suspect 1 and Suspect 2 were responsible for the bloodshed – and now he's enlisting the media and the public's help to bring them to justice. He says, 'We consider these suspects to be armed and extremely dangerous. No one should approach them. No one should attempt to apprehend them except law enforcement. It's important to emphasise that the images from Monday are indelible, and the horror of that day will remain with us for ever.'

The CCTV images capture the suspects ambling along the sidewalk, one behind the other, among the crowd who were cheering tens of thousands of exhausted runners in the final stretch of the race on Boylston Street, just two blocks away from where DesLauriers is speaking to the press now. The camera filming the press conference zooms in on an image of Suspect 1, who's wearing a black cap and shouldering a bulky backpack. Next, the lens is trained on Suspect 2. He's wearing his white baseball cap backwards, a rucksack slung over his right shoulder. The two men are thought to be associates, says DesLauriers, adding that Suspect 2 deposited the white backpack containing the second bomb 'just moments' before it exploded outside the Forum Restaurant. 'After the blast Suspect 2 was seen heading west along Boylston Street. It's unclear where Suspect 1 went.'

While urging the media to 'post, review and publicise' pictures of the suspects, DesLauriers warns: 'For clarity, these images should be the only ones – I emphasise the only ones that the public should view to assist us. Other photos should not be deemed credible and could unnecessarily divert the public's attention in the wrong direction and create undue work for vital law enforcement resources.

'For more than a hundred years the FBI has relied upon the public to be its eyes and ears. With the media's help, in an instant these images will be delivered directly into the hands of millions around the world. We know the public will play a critical role in identifying and locating these individuals.'

Immediately, the pictures – and the CCTV footage they originated from – are all over the internet. Digital news sites are updating their breaking stories by the second. Cyber traffic soars and the FBI website crashes. Twitter is rife with speculation and theories. And, of course, amateur sleuths are on the case: scrutinising – pixel by pixel – the capped men's faces, trawling social networking sites and hoping to find profile pictures resembling the two suspects. People are looking up brands of baseball caps, backpacks and jackets. They are posting hypotheses and taking virtual walks through Boston on Google Street View. The internet is awash with cyber-sleuthing sites intent on finding the Boston Marathon bombers.

Mostly, these hobbyist detectives want to help. They're adhering to the anti-vigilante rules set by administrators and have heeded DesLauriers' warning to only publicise the official photographs of the suspects. Over on the social news site Reddit, however, a witch hunt of catastrophic proportions is brewing.

The Boston Marathon is traditionally held on the third Monday in April to celebrate Patriots' Day, a state holiday in Massachusetts commemorating the first battles of the American Revolutionary War. At 2.49 p.m. on 15 April, 2013, just over four hours into the race, the celebrations in Boston turned to unthinkable terror and tragedy when the first of two bombs – a pressure cooker loaded with nails, ball bearings and explosives – detonated outside the Marathon Sports shop on Boylston Street. The ground quaked, and screams from the crowd were lost in the thundering boom. A cloud of lethal shrapnel erupted and showered the street followed by smoke. Runners and spectators were knocked off their feet in the blast that blew out all the windows in nearby buildings. Twenty-nine-year-old Krystle Marie Campbell, a restaurant manager, died in the explosion. Twelve seconds later the second pressure cooker bomb exploded outside the Forum restaurant, killing eight-year-old Martin Richard and Lingzi Lu, a twenty-three-year-old graduate student at Boston University. It was the worst terror attack on US soil since 9/11.

As devastating scenes of the blasts flashed on millions of screens around the world, Reddit users – or Redditors as they're known – bombarded the site with comments, pictures and video footage filmed during the attacks. Reddit had listed finishing times for the Boston Marathon competitors, which meant users could now gauge where individual runners were when the bombs went off – this was important information for those still waiting to hear from loved ones who'd participated in the event. This initial thread, created and moderated by Anthony Reed, then a PhD sociology student in Baton Rouge, Louisiana, saw the crowd sleuths transmitting information on casualties faster than the media could. They reported back with accounts from eyewitnesses and shared reports from major news outlets while also comparing conflicting stories on the blasts. When the *New York Post* reported the bombings had claimed twelve lives – an incorrect death toll apparently revealed to the newspaper by an unnamed New York Police Department (NYPD) officer – Anthony ditched the newspaper as a credible source on his thread.

The 2015 documentary directed by US filmmaker Greg Barker, *The Thread*, chronicles the first week of news and social media coverage following the bombing. Anthony reveals in an interview that he turned to Reddit after learning about the attack on Twitter. 'A buddy of mine posted that a bombing had occurred at the Boston Marathon. My instant thought was to go to Reddit.' Under his username, supernovasky – 'based on the Oasis song' – Anthony typed, 'There was just an explosion at the Boston Marathon. I'll use this thread for live updates.' Comments began to flood in.

'My message inbox just got blown,' Anthony recalls. 'It kept on filling up with messages. People who were actually there started sending me pictures. Comments came in – people wanting to know what had happened to loved ones and friends.' Anthony refers to a haunting image depicting medics rescuing a bloodied spectator with severed legs. The survivor, later identified as author Jeff Bauman, had been waiting to cheer his girlfriend, Erin Hurley, over the finishing line. 'We [Reddit] were definitely the first people to carry that image, before any major news organisation did. That one popped up quickly and it got a lot of people's attention. People also started posting useful information that none of the news media sites had. In my thread, people had posted runners' finishing times, so people could click on the links to see whether their friends or relatives had made it through. I felt like people were reaching out to me, but also to each other. I see a lot more humanity here [on Reddit] than I see in a lot of physical communities.'

In the documentary, Anthony explains how the site works: 'The cool thing about Reddit is that you can take every well-funded news organisation and not have to depend on just one. You can trust them at their word, or you can compare their information with people who are actually on the ground taking pictures and videos. And getting a fuller picture, which doesn't include just one source, we were able to establish exactly what had happened with precision and speed.

'By 5 p.m. on the day of the bombings, the *New York Post* was still reporting twelve dead from a NYPD source. Nobody had confirmed this figure, so we stopped using the *New York Post* as a source. It took *CNN* forty-five minutes to acknowledge the first two deaths. In the end, people didn't bother checking media sites for information – they just headed straight to Reddit.'

By late evening on 15 April, Anthony's thread had attracted a record three million followers. Grateful messages rolled in. 'Solid work, fellow Redditors,' posted one user. However, Anthony's diligent efforts soon became overshadowed by a separate, unrelated, 'subreddit' where users were going all out to identify those responsible for the massacre on Boylston Street. A media maelstrom was about to erupt. And misinformation would lead to innocent men being wrongly branded terrorists.

The subreddit, titled 'Find Boston Bombers', wormed its way online the day after the marathon bombings and, at first, its intentions seemed noble. Also interviewed in *The Thread* is aspiring screenwriter Chris Ryves. Chris was invited to moderate 'Find Boston Bombers' by the group's founder, a Redditor known only by his username OOPS777. 'I like Reddit, and I'd never moderated anything before, so I thought, "*Yeah.*" I wanted to help the Reddit community sort through this tragedy as best we could,' says Chris. 'I knew I had to put my best foot forward. Focus – treat it like a job. I thought, *"Let's not turn this discussion into something racist."'* People – still feeling the effects of 9/11 – were already talking about the possibility of the attack being the work of Islamic terrorists. In the wake of the 9/11 attacks on New York in 2001, the USA had seen an exponential rise in racially charged attacks. Chris was aware of the fragility of the situation as well as being determined to help find those responsible for the atrocities in Boston.

Embracing his moderating role with caution, Chris set out some ground rules, which he posted on the subreddit. The instructions were as follows:

1 – We do not condone vigilante justice.

2 – Do not post any personal information.

3 – Any racism will not be tolerated.

4 – Theories are welcome but make sure you fact-check your sources.

5 – Remember, we're only a subreddit. We must remember where helping ends and the work of the professionals begins.

6 – Do not make any images viral.

7 – Finally, keep in mind that most or all of these 'suspects' being discussed here are, in all likelihood, innocent people and that they should be treated as innocent until proven guilty.

'That last rule was paramount,' adds Chris. But Redditors, outraged by what they had seen in Boston, were quick to break his rules.

Thousands joined the 'Find Boston Bombers' thread, filling it with photographs of the crowds of spectators hugging the marathon's finishing line. The amateur theorists drew red circles around individuals sporting backpacks and captioned the images, asking, 'IS THIS THE BOSTON BOMBER?' They highlighted bystanders who appeared not to be focussing on the race, inferring those people were distracted by something nefarious. Some posted pictures of pressure cookers and brands of backpacks. Nicknames for possible suspects began to appear on the thread: Black Jacket Guy, Blue Duffel Bag Guy, Green Hat Guy. Redditors then homed in on two specific men amid the crowds. They named one of them Blue Robe Guy – because he had on a blue tracksuit top. Blue Robe Guy's face was clearly visible in the photograph posted on the thread. Some users suggested that his 'sagging' shoulder bag meant that something 'heavy' must be inside it. The other man, who was not given a moniker, also wore a black backpack.

The controversial message and image board website, 4chan, whose users post with total anonymity also ran the picture the Redditors had been sharing. The search for those responsible for the bombings had become a social media witch hunt. The image went viral to the point that, on 18 April, the photo of Blue Robe Guy with the other man, was splashed across the front page of the *New York Post* beneath the headline, 'Bag Men: Feds Seek These Two Pictured at Boston Marathon'.

Blue Robe Man's real name was Salaheddin Barhoum. He and his friend – the man with the black backpack – Yassine Zaimi, were *not* responsible for the bombings. They were a pair of running enthusiasts who'd gone to watch the fastest athletes finish the marathon. Appalled to find themselves implicated in the terror attacks, the two went to the police as soon as they saw their pictures being shared online – before the *Post* article was even published. The young men from Morocco were swiftly cleared of any wrongdoing. But the image still ran in the newspaper headline and the online trolls continued to splatter social media platforms with venomous threats against the men they had decided were the culprits. The editor of the *New York*

Post, Col Allan, defended his decision to print the story. He said in a statement: 'We stand by our story. The image was emailed to law enforcement agencies yesterday afternoon seeking information about these men. We did not identify them as suspects.' In a later interview with *ABC News*, Salaheddin, who was just a seventeen-year-old high school student at the time, said he feared for his life following the shocking misidentification.

To the credit of the moderators of the 'Find Boston Bomber' thread, the photograph was removed relatively quickly. But it was too late – the image was already out there. DesLauriers' decision to circulate pictures of the two men police were actually looking to speak with was, in part, to prevent another innocent person being erroneously accused of the attacks in the media or online. Releasing the CCTV photographs of the bomber suspects had been an unusual move; the tip-off might have incentivised the culprits to flee the country before their names became known. But DesLauriers stood by his decision to publish the CCTV pictures. When asked about this by correspondent Scott Pelley during a 2014 episode of CBS's *60 Minutes* news programme he responded, 'The countervailing argument is you had individuals – we had photographic evidence of individuals – who we strongly believed were responsible for the bombings and we needed to identify them as quickly as possible. These individuals could have had more bombs. They could have set those bombs off and caused carnage similar to or even greater than that of 15 April.'

The images of Suspect 1 and Suspect 2 only spurred the subreddit's hivemind into a new frenzy. Minutes after the fuzzy images went live, the page lit up with speculative posts. One user claimed to know Suspect 2. 'He went to my high school,' she wrote.

In *The Thread*, Chris describes the influx of activity as a 'huge downpour I could no longer control.' Such was the torrent of messages that Chris missed the most incriminating post to date: 'Have you considered Sunil Tripathi as a suspect?' The commenter went on to describe how Sunil had gone missing a month before the Boston Marathon. 'He's about six foot tall and weighs around 130 lbs. Just making sure we're taking everything into consideration.' This announcement blatantly violated the group's rules but amid the storm of posts battering the page at a tempo of twenty comments per minute, Chris initially missed it. If he had, it would have been deleted immediately. He says, 'It just kind of slipped by. Had I have seen it? Done. No names.'

Sunil Tripathi, was twenty-two and a philosophy student at Brown University in Providence, Rhode Island, when he disappeared on 16 March, 2013, after suspending his studies due to bouts of depression. Sunil, called Sunny by relatives and friends, had vanished suddenly from his home near the Brown campus, leaving behind his wallet, mobile phone and other belongings. In the wake of Sunil's disappearance, his distraught mum and dad, Judy and Akhil, sister Sangeeta and brother Ravi, turned to social media, making passionate appeals for the Indian-American student with a broad, sensitive smile to 'please come home.' Wrought with anxiety, they launched a Facebook page entitled 'Help Us Find Sunil Tripathi' and uploaded a cover photograph showing a laughing Sunil, his arm draped lovingly over his mother Judy's shoulder. The family had heard that missing people often track their cases online. If Sunil were to do this, they wanted him to know how much they loved and missed him.

In a moving YouTube video labelled 'For Sunny', relatives and friends appealed for him to come home, saying how much they missed his 'warm smile and generous, gentle spirit'. A heartbreaking segment of the film sees Judy telling her son, 'One of the things that I remember that I would love to do again is to lie with you on your pillow mountain.' His father, Akhil says, 'Come back, son. Call us. Love you.'

It's impossible to imagine the agony and shock the Tripathis endured seeing their dear missing boy's name brutally smeared on the very platforms they were using to search for him. After Sunil was first named, more accusatory posts appeared on the 'Find Boston Bombers' Reddit thread. Somebody had uploaded a collage twinning Sunil's picture with one of Suspect 2 and remarked on the facial similarities between the two. Other social media sites jumped on the bandwagon and, within hours, Sunil's smiling face was all over the internet. Cyber-sleuths concluded, without foundation or confirmation, that Judy and Akhil's 'gentle' son could be one of the Boston bombers.

One troll named Sunil the 'new Bin Laden' amid mounting speculation the marathon bombings were motivated by religious extremism. Others slammed Sunil's parents for 'raising a terrorist.' Vile messages of hatred and vows of retribution peppered the family's 'Help Us find Sunil Tripathi' Facebook page, forcing his family to temporarily shut down the group.

By the evening of Thursday 18 April, the Sunil rumour was trending on Twitter where more vicious untruths would spew out into the early hours of Friday. Noticing the removal of the 'Help Us Find Sunil Tripathi' Facebook page, bloggers and journalists got sucked into the viral cyclone of speculation and misconception. Some mistakenly assumed this confirmed his guilt and that Sunil's family must have frozen the site after recognising him in the images of Suspect 2. At 10.56 p.m. on Thursday, just before the Tripathis closed the page, American film blogger Sasha Stone, who runs the Awards Daily website, tweeted a link to it: 'I'm sure by now the @fbipressoffice is looking into this dude.' Then, minutes later, she followed up: 'Seconds after I sent that tweet the page is gone off of Facebook. If you can, cache it . . .'

As this frenzied hunt for the bombers raged on social media, the real Boston Marathon bombing culprits – soon to be identified as Tamerlan Tsarnaev, twenty-six, and his nineteen-year-old brother, Dzhokhar – were living in Cambridge, Massachusetts. The brothers, both Kyrgyz-American nationals of Chechen descent, had seen their pictures displayed at DesLauriers' press conference and were already talking about where to explode their remaining homemade bombs. Despite being Boston's most wanted men, the siblings decided to venture out, just hours after their pictures – Tamerlan was Suspect 1 and Dzhokhar was Suspect 2 – were beamed to the world. Their trip would turn into a night of murderous carnage ending in a bloody manhunt.

* * *

Around 10 p.m. on 18 April, the Tsarnaev brothers loaded five pipe bombs, a pressure cooker explosive, a semi-automatic handgun and a machete into Dzhokhar's Honda Civic and drove to the prestigious Massachusetts Institute of Technology (MIT) in Cambridge. That night, MIT police officer, Sean Collier, was patrolling the campus when the two men forced their way into his squad car. It's alleged Tamerlan shot Sean in the head at close range – then the brothers tried, unsuccessfully, to steal the gun harnessed to his belt. Sean died later in hospital. He was twenty-six years old.

As the killers left the murder scene, Tamerlan hijacked a Mercedes SUV, taking its terrified driver hostage at gunpoint. Pressing the gun nozzle into the side of his victim's head, Tamerlan sneered, 'Did you hear about the Boston explosion? I did that. And I just killed a cop in Cambridge.' Tamerlan ordered his captive to drive to an ATM machine, where he forced him to withdraw cash. Dzhokhar followed in the Honda Civic.

The brothers then spontaneously decided to drive to New York to 'blow-up' Times Square and 'party', but their plans were thwarted when the SUV driver managed to flee as they stopped to refuel at a petrol station in Cambridge. The driver bolted to another gas station and called the police. 'I left my cell phone in the car, so you'll be able to track them,' he told them. Police traced and gave chase to the SUV and the Honda, now headed for the Boston suburb of Watertown, about five miles west of Cambridge.

Shortly after midnight, cops spotted the SUV and the Honda Civic at the intersection of Dexter Avenue and Laurel Street in a quiet residential part of Watertown. A Wild West-style shootout ensued. Neighbours, jolted awake by the *cshh-cshh-cshh-cshh* echo of gunfire, watched from their windows. A few filmed the gunfight on their mobile phones. Dzhokhar and Tamerlan were ducked down beside the SUV, firing shots over the roof at the officers shooting back from behind a wall of parked cars – splashing sapphire light against the black sky. Through the crashing gunfire, a staticky voice blared – a call for backup over the police radio: 'We need assistance immediately. Shots fired at Watertown police officers.'

Dzhokhar and Tamerlan had only one gun but, when they'd arrived in Watertown, they'd hurriedly transferred their explosives from the Honda to the SUV, hoping to escape in it. Amid the gunfire, the brothers scrambled into the SUV, and hurled their pressure cooker and pipe bombs out of the window at the cops. 'Agents be advised. Possible dynamite type explosives. And they're throwing them at the officers responding,' was the message that came over the police communications.

Finally, Dzhokhar got behind the wheel and revved the engine as Tamerlan jumped out and calmly paced towards the police cars, gun in hand, blasting shot after shot at the cops until he ran out of ammunition. His brother slammed the accelerator, aiming for the police who scattered but smashing into Tamerlan, who was staggering after being shot. Dzhokhar then screamed the SUV into a 180-degree turn and sped off, leaving his older brother slumped and dying on the tarmac. Tamerlan, his body riddled with bullets, was ambulanced to hospital, where he died shortly afterwards. His fingerprints revealed his name to the FBI and other records told them he had a brother. The FBI believed they had finally identified the Boston Marathon bombers – and one of them was still at large.

Meanwhile, as armies of police officers searched for the second bomber, the social media fanatics were now stating as fact that Sunil Tripathi was Suspect 2. Tweeter Greg Hughes claimed he'd heard Sunil's name mentioned over the Boston Police Department's radio scanner. 'BPD scanner has identified the names,' Hughes declared. 'Suspect 1: Mike Mulugeta. Suspect 2: Sunil Tripathi.'

A train wreck of tweets followed. Anonymous, a hacking group followed by thousands, posted: 'Police on scanner identify the names of #BostonMarathon suspects in gunfight,' and went on to name Sunil. The post was retweeted over three thousand times. At 3 a.m. on Friday, 19 April, Erik Malinowski, then senior sportswriter at BuzzFeed, tweeted: 'FYI: a Facebook group dedicated to finding Sunil Tripathi, the missing Brown student, was deleted this evening.' Again, this post was retweeted by hundreds of other users, including pop-culture blogger Perez Hilton, who had over six million followers at the time. Then another BuzzFeed journalist weighed in with a further tweet referencing the alleged police scanner information. Andrew Kaczynski, today a political reporter for *CNN*, wrote: 'Wow, Reddit was right about the missing Brown student per the police scanner. Suspect identified as Sunil Tripathi.'

Television crews mobbed the Tripathis' home in Bryn Mawr, Pennsylvania. The family received sixty calls in one hour from reporters desperate for an exclusive insight into the life of the man they believed to be Suspect 2 in the Boston Marathon bombings. But Sunil Tripathi had nothing to do with the terror attacks. His name was never mentioned on the police scanner, either. Mulugeta was an unrelated person whose name was spelled out over the airwaves, but it's unclear whether he – or she – exists. The first name, Mike, remains unconfirmed. The cyber detectives – and subsequently the mainstream media – had got it all horribly wrong.

Meanwhile, still on the run from law enforcement, Dzhokhar abandoned the SUV nearby then fled on foot. A manhunt involving hundreds of police officers and FBI agents led to Dzhokhar's capture on the evening of 19 April. Officers found him, covered with blood and hiding inside a dry-docked boat in a resident's garden.

Ironically, given the frenzy and the tragic cases of mistaken identity that had been carried out on social media, the Boston Police Department announced Dzhokhar Tsarnaev's arrest on Twitter. The celebratory tweet read: 'CAPTURED!!! The hunt is over. The search is done. The terror is over. And justice has won. Suspect in custody.' Minutes later, the department sent this message in memory of those killed by the bombers. 'In our time of rejoicing, let us not forget the families of Martin Richard, Lingzi Lu, Krystle Campbell and Officer Sean Collier.'

As soon as the FBI publicly named Tamerlan and Dzhokhar Tsarnaev, the camera crews retreated from the Tripathis' doorstep. For the mainstream media, the fact that Sunil had been wrongfully singled out as a suspect wasn't as newsworthy as the idea that he was a terrorist. His family posted a poignant statement on a social media group, urging supporters to help them find him. 'A tremendous and painful amount of attention has been cast on our beloved Sunil Tripathi in the past twelve hours,' they wrote. 'Now, more than ever, our greatest strength comes from your enduring support. We thank all of you who have reached out to our family and ask that you continue to raise awareness and to help us find our gentle, loving, and thoughtful Sunil.'

The 'Find Boston Bombers' group rapidly removed the posts about Sunil and pleaded with the media to stop sharing the damaging information. In an apology to Sunil's family, Chris Ryves wrote: 'I'd like to extend the deepest apologies to the family of Sunil Tripathi for any part we may have had in relaying what has turned out to be faulty information. We cannot begin to know what you're going through and for that we are truly sorry. Several users, twitter users, and other sources had heard him identified as the suspect and believed it to be confirmed. We were mistaken.'

But the nightmare continued for the Tripathi family. Less than a week after the hunt for the Boston bombers ended, they learned that their beloved Sunny wouldn't be coming home. His body was found floating in the Seekonk River in Providence on 23 April. Sunil's relatives confirmed he'd committed suicide but he did not end his life because of the shocking allegations made against him. It's believed he died before the marathon bombings happened. His family told of their 'indescribable grief' on their reinstated Facebook page. Despite the added trauma they'd suffered with the accusations hurled at their Sunny, the Tripathis' dignified post displayed no malice towards those who'd jumped to such cataclysmic conclusions. Thanking people who'd sent prayers and messages from all corners of the world, they added, 'Take care of one another. Be gentle, be compassionate.'

The disastrous online investigation carried out by amateur sleuths into the Boston Marathon bomber suspects is a prime example of how overzealous sleuths can sometimes cause more harm than good. It was not just that internet sleuths were too quick to jump to conclusions but that professional journalists were too. In the fiercely competitive race to be the first news outlet to break the story, basic fact-checking went out of the window. The FBI had even sent a cutting warning to the media in the wake of the bombings – before those news organisations falsely identified Sunil. The agency's statement on 17 April, 2013, said: 'Over the past day and a half there has been a number of press reports based on information from unofficial sources that has been inaccurate. Since these stories often have unintended consequences, we ask the media, particularly at this early stage of the investigation, to exercise caution and attempt to verify information through appropriate official channels before reporting.' For Sunil's family, unfortunately, much as they continue to try to separate him from the allegations, it's impossible to do so. Online, he's remembered as the man wrongly labelled a Boston Marathon bomber.

Four years later, similar mistakes were made in the hours following the Westminster Bridge terror attack in London. News organisations again followed social media reports that misidentified the culprit. Five people were killed, and fifty others were injured when a man ploughed his car into pedestrians on the bridge before abandoning his vehicle and stabbing policeman Keith Palmer to death outside the Houses of Parliament.

Hours after the attack on 22 March 2017, online detectives named the attacker as Abu Izzadeen, a radical British cleric who was in prison at the time on terrorism charges. Soon, the news spread on Twitter and Facebook. A Russian news site posted a fake picture of Izzadeen, which was also circulated on social media. Then, based on the Twitter reports – plus a tip from a separate source – *Channel 4 News* ran the story on their live show, naming Izzadeen as the suspect who was shot dead by police at the scene. *The Independent* followed *Channel 4's* lead, but later deleted their online report. Izzadeen's Wikipedia page was updated, naming him as the Westminster Bridge terrorist. The real attacker was identified the following day as British-born Khalid Masood, a violent criminal with a string of convictions spanning twenty years.

The police have long relied on the public's assistance in solving crimes, and have long encouraged people to forward information to tip lines or respond to witness appeals. And, if done sensibly, law enforcement welcomes the good work of citizen sleuths, as we've learned in this book. But, as retired Toronto homicide detective Mark Mendelson points out, the internet can be a dangerous place when inexperienced armchair detectives decide to take the law into their own hands or spread unsubstantiated theories online. These activities can seriously hinder a police investigation or even hurt innocent people.

'One of the dangers with technology is that millions of people around the world have now become super sleuths,' Mark explains. 'They read about murder or watch a crime documentary on TV and immediately begin searching. They search social sites and dating sites and start putting their findings together – chats and blogs where they compare notes and theories and motives. Question is, what do they do with these conclusions? The danger is they'll do something on their own or as a group. Ideally what they should be doing is calling police with this information.'

Mark provided live commentary for Toronto's *CTV News* channel during the FBI's manhunt for Dzhokhar. He didn't know about the media storm surrounding Sunil at that point as his focus was on the police investigation, but he later read about how the student had been unjustly vilified. 'The problem is people start looking at pictures online. In this case, Sunny was missing – he may never have been implicated otherwise. But people make their own determinations. They see a picture and think, "*Oh, that must be the guy,*" so they put that information on social media without due diligence or investigation or confirmation behind it. And of course, once that person hits the enter button on their keyboard, it's gone. Before you know it, wrong pictures of individuals are around the world at the push of a button.

'The only people who should be putting out suspect information – descriptions, names, pictures or security video footage should be the police. But quasi journos, wannabe journos, wannabe detectives draw their own conclusions, and these misidentifications take on their own lives. They grow exponentially and you just can't put the genie back in the bottle.

'Boston Police would not have noticed the scanner tweet. They were concentrating on finding the bombers. There were other murders – one of their cops had been shot dead. They don't have the time or resources to quash every misidentification that's out there on the internet. Meanwhile, some innocent person faces a barrage of demonstrators and reporters outside their home. It's dangerous. That person can get hurt before they even get the chance to clear their name. They could get shot or stabbed. Or they might even take – or attempt to take – their life.'

Mark's last words are hauntingly resonant when it comes to one case where a group of online sleuths tried to solve a disappearance and subsequent death of a young woman visiting Los Angeles.

Elisa Lam, a twenty-one-year-old student from Vancouver, arrived in the US in January 2013 to start a long-planned solo trip up the Californian coast. She checked into the Cecil Hotel, a few blocks away from crime-ridden Skid Row in downtown Los Angeles, seemingly unaware of the building's volatile and violent history. The monstrous fourteen-floor hotel had opened in 1924 and then rapidly declined during the Great Depression.

Down at heel, the cheap, grubby rooms were made available for weekly or monthly stays, and the Cecil became a haven for sex workers, drug addicts and transients. At least sixteen deaths have been recorded at the hotel. Serial killer Richard Ramirez stayed in a $14 per night room on the top floor of the Cecil before his capture in 1985 and reportedly dumped his bloodied clothes in a bin outside the hotel after murdering one of his victims. Austrian serial killer Jack Unterweger also stayed in the hotel in 1991 to pay homage to Ramirez.

Elisa, who suffered from bipolar disorder, was reported missing after she failed to check out of the Cecil on 1 February, 2013. She had left her luggage, ID and medication behind in her room. Police and sniffer dogs searched the hotel and scoured nearby streets but found nothing. Two weeks later, with no leads to work with, Los Angeles Police Department (LAPD) released unsettling footage of Elisa's last known sighting at the Cecil, filmed by a CCTV camera inside an elevator. In the four-minute clip, Elisa walks into the elevator, presses some buttons then retreats to the corner. The elevator doors remain open and, seconds later, Elisa shuffles into the corridor and moves her feet in a square motion before going back inside. She jabs more buttons on the column, then darts into the hall again. In the last frame Elisa is turning her hands in the air, as though gesticulating at somebody further along the corridor. She then steps out of view. The elevator doors close and, when they reopen seconds later, there's nobody outside.

The elevator video went viral and amateur sleuths swamped the internet – and police – with their thoughts on the footage. They posted opinions on Reddit and uploaded videos to YouTube, scrutinising Elisa's erratic behaviour and questioning the authenticity of the surveillance film. Some suggested Elisa was playing a Korean elevator game – a ritual of pressing an elevator's buttons in a certain order to reach another dimension. Elisa twisted her foot in the final frame – was she fleeing a pursuer? Based on the Cecil's creepy background, some armchair detectives theorised Elisa had fallen prey of evil spirits haunting the building. Many believed the video had been edited, possibly as part of a cover-up by the hotel or police.

Six days after police released the bizarre clip, former maintenance worker, Santiago Lopez found Elisa's naked body floating inside one of the four thousand-gallon cisterns atop the Cecil Hotel. Santiago had gone to check the tanks after guests complained the running water had turned brown and tasted 'foul.'

The Los Angeles County Coroner's Office ruled Elisa had accidentally drowned in the tank. Mental illness being a significant contributing factor in her death. Elisa had suffered hallucinations in the past when she neglected to take prescribed medication for her bipolar condition. The online theorists didn't think it could be so simple. Hotel staff had told reporters that the tank was awkward to reach and could only be accessed via a ten-foot ladder. Getting into the cistern would require lifting a nine-kilogram lid – and Santiago claimed the lid was open when he discovered Elisa face-up in the tank. How could a slight young woman like Elisa possibly heave that lid open and just jump in? Suspecting foul play, they tried to retrace Elisa's last steps. '*Who was she gesturing at in the elevator footage? Is that somebody else's foot in the video?*' And the deeper they delved into the mystery the more their musings mushroomed into outlandish speculations.

It transpired that there had been an outbreak of tuberculosis in Skid Row around the time of Elisa's death and this roused Redditors' suspicions – especially when they learned that the test for the specific strain of the disease was named LAM-ELISA (an abbreviation for Lipoarabinomannan (LAM) Enzyme-Linked Immunosorbent Assay (ELISA)). In a Reddit thread, users suggested Elisa was a test subject for a new tuberculosis drug and had experienced wild side effects from the medication. Or maybe Elisa was a human biological weapon who had been sent to LA to spread the malaise?

Online communities even turned to the movies for clues, proposing Elisa was the victim of a copycat killer inspired by the supernatural horror film *Dark Water*. In the 2005 film, a girl's body is found in a water tank topping an apartment block after residents noticed the water looked dark and tasted weird.

The death of Elisa Lam became one of the most talked-about cases on the internet. But a group of sleuthers' obsessive insistence that *somebody* had killed Elisa and dumped her body in the tank would nearly destroy an innocent man's life.

The web detectives stumbled across a video a Mexican metal band artist known as Morbid – real name Pablo Vergara – had made of himself inside a room at the Cecil Hotel. The footage was a teaser for Morbid's latest music video for his song titled 'Died in Pain'. The song's lyrics referenced a woman drowning in water. Morbid had uploaded the video to his YouTube channel a few days after Elisa's body was discovered, which seemed too coincidental for the internet mob to ignore. Exploring Morbid's YouTube channel, it became apparent to some sleuthers that he had an obsession with death and serial killers. In one video, Morbid performs against a backdrop plastered with images of Ted Bundy and the Black Dahlia murder victim Elizabeth Short – who was reportedly last seen at the Cecil Hotel before her death in 1947.

Based on this alone, the internet groups began to discuss and spread their presumptions online, with many going so far as publicly labelling Morbid a killer. They attacked his social media accounts, got his music deleted from YouTube and circulated his photograph. They even tipped off a Taiwanese news station, which then named Morbid as an official suspect.

If Morbid's accusers had checked their facts, they would have learned that he filmed his Cecil Hotel video a year previously – and that he was in Mexico at the time of Elisa's death. Alas, the damage had already been done. In the 2021 Netflix docuseries *The Vanishing at the Cecil Hotel*, which chronicles Elisa's disappearance and death, Morbid describes how he had a breakdown after receiving a barrage of death threats. He stopped making music in the wake of the false allegations and even attempted suicide. At one point, the federal police of Mexico came to his door to ask if he'd ever made 'blood sacrifices.' Morbid says in the documentary, 'There were just false accusations, death threats, every day. There was no escape. I tried to take my life and I woke up in a psychiatric hospital. I lost my freedom of expression. At a point, when you get so much hate and just negativity, there's something that breaks in your mind. Something clicks.' Morbid adds that he's trying to rebuild his life but will always be haunted by the cyberbullying. 'It sucks every day.'

I spoke to some of my interviewees for this book about the negative impact irresponsible online sleuthing has on the rest of the community. Websleuths' Tricia Griffith was appalled at the cyberbullying against Morbid. It was her forum that initially came under attack after the Netflix series. The documentary makers had used the label 'websleuths' to describe the mob that came after Morbid. Tricia explains: 'In the series they used the text "websleuth" as a generic term for their interviewees. So, when that poor man starts talking about how "websleuths" ruined his life, people thought it was us who had harassed him. Oh my God, I was so mad. Websleuths is trademarked by me. I put the word out there that the campaign had nothing to do with Websleuths. I wrote to Netflix, I did *everything*.

'When the Morbid story emerged, we shut down our Elisa Lam thread. We would not let anybody discuss him. Morbid had nothing to do with Elisa's death and the internet sleuths responsible [for the campaign against Morbid] make it difficult for the rest of us who are abiding by the 'no naming and shaming' rules. Cases like this – and that of poor Sunil Tripathi's misidentification – give our community a bad name.'

But even the most seasoned sleuths admit they've made mistakes along the way. Todd Matthews knows, in hindsight, he shouldn't have cold-called Rosemary Westbrook when he spotted her message about her missing sister, who turned out to be Tent Girl. 'Contacting victims, families, or suspects in an open case should be avoided at all costs,' he says. 'This is exactly what we warn new cyber-sleuths not to do. Just one phone call could jeopardise an active investigation, drive away potential witnesses or re-victimise those affected by the case. I was wrong to call Rosemary, but I didn't know any better back then. I was a naïve kid and cyber-sleuthing didn't really exist. I took Rosemary's message at face value. Maybe I should have contacted the sheriff first, but I didn't know whether there was enough information there for him to pursue the case. I learned a valuable lesson early on.'

With thirty-five years' sleuthing experience now under his belt, Todd has a wealth of advice to offer wannabe citizen detectives. When trying to match an unidentified victim to a missing person, for example, do not make 'wild guesses.' He advises focussing on the Doe's distinctive features, such as tattoos or noticeable dental features – like his Campbell County Jane Doe #2's husk tooth. 'If you can go to the authorities and say, "Here are three cases I've found where the missing person has similar features to the Doe," then police can move on that information,' he says.

Much of Todd's work with the Doe Network nowadays is ensuring hard copy files are digitised – because you 'can't google a filing cabinet.' He still embraces traditional research methods too: 'Don't underestimate low-tech resources. I have found cases in old newspapers that law enforcement didn't even know were still open. Not everything is online.'

Good citizen detectives will forward all information they uncover to law enforcement, but they should not expect glory for doing so. As Todd concludes: 'If you're in it for the credit, then you're here for the wrong reason. The Doe Network is all about the victims. If you genuinely want to help victims and families and honestly care about finding justice for them, then you'll make a good citizen detective.'

Wise words worth heeding, I'd say, from the world's first internet sleuth.

Useful Resources

A&E true crime blog – by the A&E television network (aetv.com/real-crime) that specialises in true crime documentaries. The blog features articles on murder cases, serial killers and interviews with people featured in the channel's shows.

Ancestry.com – American genealogy company that runs a network of thirty billion genealogical and historical records. The company has sold eighteen million DNA testing kits to customers.

Classmates.com – a US social networking site founded in 1995 that helps users connect with former schoolfriends and view past class yearbooks.

CODIS – FBI's Combined DNA Index System, which archives and compares DNA profiles obtained from crime scenes, unidentified bodies, missing people and convicted criminals. CODIS enables local and federal forensic crime labs to work together to solve crimes between jurisdictions.

Corel Photo-Paint – a digital photo-editing package used by forensic artists. The high-quality graphics package features a host of realistic special effects, from retouching to photo-painting.

DNA Doe Project – founded in 2017 by crime-mystery novelist Margaret Press and forensic genealogist Dr Colleen Fitzpatrick, the non-profit US-based organisation is making global headlines for its ground-breaking work. The project's network of dedicated volunteers uses forensic genealogy to 'name' unidentified Jane and John Does, working alongside law-enforcement agencies. So far, the DNA Doe Project has named over seventy-five Does. Volunteers come from an array of backgrounds.

Doe Network – founded by Todd Matthews, Jennifer Marra and Helene Wahlstrom in 1999. The volunteer-run organisation is devoted to assisting investigating agencies in bringing closure to worldwide cold cases involving missing and unidentified people. As stated on Doe Network website's homepage: 'It is our mission to give the nameless back their names and return the missing to their families.' The Doe Network has identified over 100 Jane and John Does and has gathered data to keep thousands of similar cases in the public eye.

Florida Unidentified Decedents Database (FLUIDDB.com) – a clearinghouse containing information about unidentified remains found in Florida. The site includes a public search facility.

ForumsForJustice.org – an online forum founded by Websleuths. com owner, Tricia Griffith, in the late 1990s which is still active. Focusing on the JonBenét Ramsey case, the group aims to discredit scandalous accusations made against innocent suspects while highlighting those who were never thoroughly investigated.

GEDmatch – a commercial genealogy database where people can enter their raw DNA data from consumer genetic testing companies like 23andMe and Ancestry.com to compare with others and find relatives. GEDmatch gained headlines in April 2018 when law enforcement used the database to identify Golden State Killer, Joseph DeAngelo, in California. The following year, GEDmatch tightened its privacy rules by asking users to 'opt in' to share data with law enforcement.

Google Earth Outreach – this resource hosts several tutorials on subjects such as creating image overlays, navigating satellite images and how to save unique camera angles to placemark locations.

Measure app – turn your device into a tape measure with this app, which gauges the size of real objects, a person's height and automatically calculates dimensions of rectangular objects.

National Center for Missing and Exploited Children (NCMEC) – an information clearing house and US national resource centre relating to victims and missing and exploited children. The NCMEC focuses on locating missing kids and also identifying deceased children, teenagers and young adults via forensic facial reconstructions.

National Crime Information Center (NCIC) database – the computerised index, listing missing people and criminal data, allows law-enforcement agencies across America to exchange information.

National Missing and Unidentified Persons System (NamUs) – pronounced 'Name us'. The US Department of Justice system manages an online database of records detailing unidentified bodies, cross-referenced to missing people files. NamUs supports families impacted by the death or disappearance of a loved one, and provides free forensic resources such as fingerprint examination, odontology, anthropology and DNA analysis. Anyone can register case information on the database.

Project EDAN – an acronym for 'Everyone Deserves a Name' was founded by citizen detective Todd Matthews in February 2001. Working with a group of volunteer certified forensic artists, Todd's vision is to 'give faces to the faceless' by creating composite sketches and clay reconstructions of unidentified victims, based on autopsy photographs and skulls.

TinEye Reverse Image – a search engine for tracing the origin of pictures.

Uncovered – this website, uncovered.com, is a place for citizen sleuths to come together to share theories on cases. Uncovered says it's building a software platform to 'combine data, analytics and the wisdom of the community' to help solve cold cases of murdered and missing people. The group offers a host of tips to wannabe sleuths, including downloadable documents, including a free 'Citizen Detective Guide'.

Wayback Machine – this is the best website for internet archiving, allowing users to search over 168 billion past websites, which is handy when researching cold cases.

Websleuths.com – this citizen sleuth Tricia Griffith's crime blogging site, which she bought in 2004. Tightly moderated with a strict 'no rumours' policy, the forum today has 200,000 members who converge online to discuss and investigate unsolved crimes, and cold and missing person cases. The international network comprises an impressive smorgasbord of experts, from office workers to nurses, doctors, surgeons, retired law-enforcement officers, ink specialists, psychologists and psychiatrists. Tricia also hosts live Websleuths videos on her YouTube channel.

Nalini Singh was born in Fiji and raised in New Zealand. She spent three years living and working in Japan, and travelling around Asia before returning to New Zealand.

She has worked as a lawyer, a librarian, a candy factory general hand, a bank temp and an English teacher, not necessarily in that order.

Learn more about her and her novels at:
www.nalinisingh.com